HAMILTON BEACH INDOOR GRILL COOKBOOK

+160 AFFORDABLE, DELICIOUS AND HEALTHY RECIPES THAT ANYONE CAN COOK. COOKING SMOKELESS AND LESS MESS FOR BEGINNERS AND ADVANCED USERS.

DANA REED

CONTENTS

BREAKFAST RECIPES

BEEF AND PORK RECIPES

POULTRY RECIPES

FISH & SEAFOOD RECIPES

VEGETARIAN & VEGGIE RECIPES

SALAD RECIPES

SANDWICH RECIPES

SIDE DISHES RECIPES

SNACK RECIPES

DESSERT RECIPES

EXTRA RECIPES

BREAKFAST RECIPES

1

SAUSAGE AND MUSHROOM BREAKFAST SKEWERS

Preparation Time: 8-10 minutes

Cooking Time: 4 minutes

Servings: 4

Ingredients:

•2 Italian Sausage Links

•4 Whole White Button Mushrooms

•1 Red Bell Pepper

•Salt and Pepper, to taste

Method:

1.Soak four skewers in cold water for 2-3 minutes.

2.Preheat your grill to 375 degrees F.

3.Meanwhile, cut each sausage in eight pieces.

4.Quarter the mushrooms and cut the red pepper into eight pieces.

5.Sprinkle the mushrooms and pepper generously with salt and pepper.

6.Grab the skewers and thread the ingredients – sausage, mushroom, pepper, sausage mushroom, sausage mushroom, pepper, sausage, mushroom, in that order.

7.Place onto the grill and lower the lid.

8.Cook for 4 minutes closed.

9.Serve alongside some bread and a favorite spread and enjoy.

Nutritional Value:

•Calories 118
•Total Fats 9.1g
•Carbs 4g
•Protein 7.3g
•Fiber: 0.6g

2

GRILLED HAM OMELET

Preparation Time: 5 minutes
  Cooking Time: 5 minutes
  Servings: 2
  Ingredients:
  •6 Eggs
  •2 Ham Slices, chopped
  •2 tbsp chopped Herbs by choice
  •¼ tsp Onion Powder
  •1 tbsp minced Red Pepper
  •¼ tsp Garlic Powder
  •Salt and Pepper, to taste
  Method:
  1.Preheat your grill to 350 degrees F.
  2.In the meantime, whisk the eggs in a bowl and add the rest of the ingredients to it. Stir well to combine.
  3.Open the grill and unlock the hinge.
  4.Coat the griddle with some cooking spray and gently pour the egg mixture onto it.
  5.With a silicone spatula, mix the omelet as you would in a skillet.

6.When it reaches your desired consistency, divide among two serving plates.

7.Enjoy!

Nutritional Value:

•Calories 271

•Total Fats 17.5g

•Carbs 2.4g

•Protein 24g

•Fiber: 0.1g

MEXICAN EGGS ON HAYSTACKS

Preparation Time: 10 minutes

Cooking Time: 12 minutes

Servings: 6

Ingredients:

•½ cup Breadcrumbs

•3 ½ cups Store-Bought Hash Browns

•2/3 cup Sour Cream

•2 tsp Tex Mex Seasoning

•6 Eggs

•1/3 cup shredded Cheddar

•Salt and Pepper, to taste

Method:

1.Preheat your grill to medium.

2.In the meantime, squeeze the hash browns to get rid of excess water, and place in a bowl.

3.Add the breadcrumbs, cheese, half of the Tex-Mex, and season with some salt and pepper.

4.Mix with your hands to combine.

5.Open the grill, unlock the hinge for the griddle, and lay it open. Spray with cooking spray.

6.Make six patties out of the hash brown mixture and arrange onto the griddle.

7.Cook for 7 minutes, flipping once, halfway through. Tarsnsfer to six serving plates.

8.Crack the eggs open onto the griddle, season with salt and pepper, and cook until they reach your preferred consistency.

9.Top the hash browns with the egg.

10. Combine the sourcream and remaining Tex Mex and top the eggs with it.

11. Enjoy!

Nutritional Value:

•Calories 340

•Total Fats 21g

•Carbs 25g

•Protein 8.2g

•Fiber: 2g

4

HARISSA AVOCADO SAUSAGE AND EGG BREAKFAST PANINI

This Panini is filled with Mediterranean flavor. The Harissa and pepper jack give this some heat, the arugula provides a peppery flavor, and the Merguez has a beautiful spiced flavor.

Prep Time: 15 Minutes

Cook Time: 6 Minutes

Servings: 2

Ingredients:

4 pieces of sourdough or crusty bread

¼ cup Harissa

2 eggs

½ avocado, sliced into pieces

1 cup pepper jack cheese

A handful of arugula

2 Merguez sausages, cooked

Olive oil

2 tsp butter

Directions:

• Use a whisk to beat the egg with a pinch of salt and pepper. Place the butter in a skillet and melt it on medium heat. Use a spoon to stir the eggs and push them across the pan. Cook until the eggs set, about 1 to 2 minutes.

- Chop the sausage into small pieces or butterfly them. Spread the Harissa on what's going to be the inside of two pieces of bread. Put a layer of egg on the Harissa side of the 2 pieces of bread, then the sausage, then the arugula, then avocado and top with the cheese. Then place the other two pieces of bread on top of the cheese. Brush the top and bottom of the sandwiches with olive oil.

- Cook the Panini on medium heat for 4 to 6 minutes, flipping halfway through. The bread should be toasted, and the cheese should be melted.

5

CORN CAKES WITH SALSA AND CREAM CHEESE

Preparation Time: 8 minutes

Cooking Time: 8 minutes

Servings: 8

Ingredients:

•½ cup Cornmeal

•¼ cup Butter, melted

•½ cup Salsa

•14 ounces canned Corn, drained

•1 cup Milk

•6 ounces Cream Cheese

•1 ½ cups Flour

•6 Eggs

•¼ cup chopped Spring Onions

•1 tsp Baking Powder

•Salt and Pepper, to taste

Method:

1.In a bowl, whisk together the eggs, butter, cream cheese, and milk.

2.Whisk in the cornmeal, flour, baking powder, salt, and pepper.

3.Fold in the remaining ingredients and stir well to incorporate.

4.Preheat your grill to medium.

5.When the light is on, unlock the hinge and lower to your counter.

6.Spray the griddle with a nonstick spray.

7.Ladle the batter onto the griddle (about ¼ of cup per cake).

8.When the cakes start bubbling, flip them over and cook until golden brown.

9.Serve as desired and enjoy!

Nutritional Value:
•Calories 325
•Total Fats 15g
•Carbs 35g
•Protein 11g
•Fiber: 3g

6

BALSAMIC VINEGAR & GARLIC BRUSCHETTA

This part-perfect appetizer will have your friends asking for this wonderful recipe that will be the hit at any party for friends or family.

Prep Time: 10 Minutes

Cook Time: 3-5 Minutes

Servings: 6-8

Ingredients:

8 diced tomatoes

1/3 cup chopped fresh basil

1/4 cup shredded Parmesan cheese

2 cloves garlic, minced

1 tbsp. balsamic vinegar

1 tsp. olive oil

1/4 tsp. kosher salt

1/4 tsp. freshly ground black pepper

1 loaf French bread, toasted and sliced

Directions:

• Toss together in a bowl or container the tomatoes, basil, Parmesan cheese, and garlic.

- Combine the balsamic vinegar, olive oil, kosher salt, and pepper.
- Place the bread slices on panini press grill for 2 about minutes until toasted and set it aside.
- You will now serve the toast and take the mixture to be spread on the toasted bread .
- Enjoy

7

DELICIOUS CHOCOLATE BACON BRUSCHETTA

We mentioned that bacon goes good on almost anything and this is one of those dishes you just have to try for yourself. A taste but twister for sure!!

Prep Time: 10 Minutes

Cook Time: 5 Minutes

Servings: 4-5

Ingredients

4 slices bacon

9 thin slices of sourdough baguette

olive oil, or as needed

3 ounces miniature chocolate chips

Directions

• Cook bacon over medium heat until crisp in a pan or skillet. You can also cook the bacon in your Panini press if desired.

• Drain the bacon on a paper towel of some sort. When it cools, crumble the bacon.

• Brush both sides of the bread with oil.

• Mix crumbled bacon with chocolate chips in a bowl and top each baguette slice with a small amount of the mixture.

• Place the bread slices on panini press grill and pull down till the top is about 1 inch from the chocolate bread slices. Heat for about 2 minutes until the chocolate chips are soft but still firm.

• Enjoy!

CHOCOLATE CHIP AND BLUEBERRY PANCAKES

Preparation Time: 5 minutes

Cooking Time: 5 minutes

Servings: 2

Ingredients:

• 1 cup Pancake Mix

• ¼ cup Orange Juice

• 1/3 cup Fresh Blueberries

• ¼ cup Chocolate Chips

• ½ cup Water

Method:

1. Preheat your grill to medium.

2. Meanwhile, combine the pancake mix with the orange juice and water.

3. Fold in the chocolate chips and blueberries.

4. Open the grill, unhinge, and lay the griddle onto your counter.

5. Spray with cooking spray.

6. Add about 1/6 of the batter at a time, to the griddle.

7. Cook until bubbles start forming on the surface, then flip over, and cook until the other side turns golden brown.

8.Serve and enjoy!

Nutritional Value:

•Calories 370

•Total Fats 9g

•Carbs 66g

•Protein 3g

•Fiber: 3g

QUICK OAT & BANANA PANCAKES

Preparation Time: 8 minutes

Cooking Time: 5 minutes

Servings: 4

Ingredients:

•½ cup Oats

•¼ cup chopped Nuts by choice (Walnuts and Hazelnuts work best)

•1 large Ripe Banana, chopped finely

•2 cups Pancake Mix

Method:

1.Preheat your grill to medium and unlock the hinge. Open it flat on your counter.

2.Meanwhile, prepare the pancake mix according to the instruction on the package.

3.Stir in the remaining ingredients well.

4.Spray the griddle with some cooking spray.

5.Drop about ¼ cup onto the griddle.

6.Cook for a minute or two, just until the pancake begins to puff up.

7.Flip over and cook for another minute or so – the recipe makes about 16 pancakes.

8.Serve as desired and enjoy!

Nutritional Value:

•Calories 310
•Total Fats 8g
•Carbs 56g
•Protein 14g
•Fiber: 8g

GOAT CHEESE PESTO AND EGG ENGLISH MUFFIN PANINI

This Panini features some lovely contrasting flavors. The goat cheese has a strong flavor that's tempered by the aromatic flavor of the peso, and the rich flavor of the eggs. If you're not a fan of goat cheese try using half as much goat cheese or no goat cheese at all! It's truly a treat anyway you decide to make it!

Prep Time: 20 Minutes

Cook Time: 5 Minutes

Servings: 4

Ingredients:

4 eggs

4 English muffins, split and lightly toasted

4 tbsps. prepared pesto

4 oz. Humboldt Fog goat cheese or Bucheron de chevre, sliced into 4 rounds

4 large tomato slices

8 leaves radicchio

Olive oil

4 tsp butter

Directions:

• Use a whisk to beat the eggs with a pinch of salt and pepper.

Place the butter in a skillet and melt it on medium heat. Use a spoon to stir the eggs and push them across the pan. Cook until the eggs set, about 1 to 2 minutes.

• Spread the pesto on the inside of part of the English muffins, then layer the eggs on the inside of the lower piece of the English muffin, then the cheese, then the radicchio, then the tomatoes, and top with the other half of the English muffin. Brush the top and bottom of the sandwiches with olive oil.

• Cook the Panini on medium heat for 4 to 5 minutes, flipping halfway through. The English muffin should be toasted, and the cheese should be melted.

11

FRENCH TOAST AND STRAWBERRIES IN CREAM PANINI

This Panini will a huge hit with your kids. The cream cheese mixes perfectly with the strawberries as a delicious surprise in the middle of two delicious pieces of French toast!

Prep Time: 20 Minutes

Cook Time: 6 Minutes

Servings: 4

Ingredients:

6 large eggs

1 cup whole milk

1/2 cup heavy cream

1/4 cup fresh orange juice (from about 1 medium orange)

2 tbsps. vanilla extract

2 tbsps. cognac (optional)

2 tbsps. granulated sugar

1/2 tsp ground cinnamon

Pinch of freshly grated nutmeg

Salt

8 slices Texas toast or other thick white bread

1/2 cup cream cheese

1/2 cup of strawberries, sliced thinly + 1/4 cup strawberries cut into small pieces

Confectioners' sugar, for garnish

Pure maple syrup, for garnish

Directions:

• Spread the cream cheese on what's going to be the inside of the pieces of bread and then place the strawberries on top of 4 of them. Top with the remaining pieces of bread.

• Use a whisk to combine the eggs, milk, cream, orange juice, cognac, sugar, cinnamon, and vanilla. Put the sandwiches in a shallow baking dishes and cover with the mixture you just created. Allow the sandwiches to rest in the mixture for 10 min.

• Preheat your flip sandwich maker on medium high heat.

• Cook the Panini for 6 to 7 minutes in your preheated flap sandwiched maker, flipping halfway through.

• Top with confectioners' sugar and maple syrup

MIXED BERRY FRENCH TOAST PANINI

This Panini has all the berry flavor you can handle. The creaminess of the cream cheese enhances the flavors of the raspberries and blackberries. Use frozen berries if you can't find fresh ones, but make sure to thaw them out first.

Prep Time: 20 Minutes
Cook Time: 6 Minutes
Servings: 4

Ingredients:

6 large eggs
1 cup whole milk
1/2 cup heavy cream
1/4 cup fresh orange juice (from about 1 medium orange)
2 tbsps. vanilla extract
2 tbsps. cognac (optional)
2 tbsps. granulated sugar
1/2 tsp ground cinnamon
Pinch of freshly grated nutmeg
Pinch of salt
8 slices Texas toast or other thick white bread
1 cup blackberries

1 cup raspberries

Confectioners' sugar, for garnish

Pure maple syrup, for garnish

Directions:

• Spread the cream cheese on what's going to be the inside of the pieces of bread and then place the strawberries on top of 4 of them. Top with the remaining pieces of bread.

• Use a whisk to combine the eggs, milk, cream, orange juice, cognac, sugar, cinnamon, and vanilla. Put the sandwiches in a shallow baking dishes and cover with the mixture you just created. Allow sandwiches to rest in the mixture for 10 minutes.

• Preheat your flip sandwich maker on medium high heat.

• Cook the Panini for 6 to 7 minutes in your preheated flap sandwiched maker, flipping halfway through.

• Top with confectioners' sugar and maple syrup.

13

FRENCH TOAST AND GRILLED BANANA PANINI

This Panini is a banana lover's dream. The perfectly caramelized bananas are only enhanced by the wonderful flavor of the French toast, creating a sandwich everyone in your family will love!

Prep Time: 20 Minutes

Cook Time: 6 Minutes

Servings: 4

Ingredients:

6 large eggs

1 cup whole milk

1/2 cup heavy cream

1/4 cup fresh orange juice

2 tbsps. vanilla extract

2 tbsps. cognac (optional)

2 tbsps. granulated sugar

1/2 tsp ground cinnamon

Pinch of freshly grated nutmeg

Salt

8 slices Texas toast or other thick white bread

3 large ripe bananas

2 tbsps. unsalted butter, melted

Confectioners' sugar, for garnish

Pure maple syrup, for garnish

Directions:

• Use a whisk to combine the eggs, milk, cream, orange juice, cognac, sugar, cinnamon, and vanilla. Put the bread in a couple of shallow baking dishes and cover with the mixture you just created. Allow the bread to rest in the mixture for 10 minutes

• While the bread is resting preheat a skillet on medium heat. Then coat the bananas with melted butter and cook them in the skillet until are nice and brown all over, about 3 minutes. They should be releasing their juices. When bananas have cooled down a little chop them into chunks.

• Preheat your flip sandwich maker on medium high heat. While that's preheating place the bananas on half the pieces of bread and top with the other pieces of bread.

• Cook the Panini for 6 to 7 minutes in your preheated flap sandwiched maker, flipping halfway through.

• Top with confectioners' sugar and maple syrup

14

CLASSIC BACON AND EGGS BREAKFAST

Preparation Time: 2 minutes

Cooking Time: 8 minutes

Servings: 1

Ingredients:

•2 Eggs

•2 Bacon Slices

•2 Bread Slices

•Salt and Pepper, to taste

Method:

1.Preheat your grill to 400 degrees F, and make sure that the kickstand is in position.

2.When the light goes on, add the bacon to the plate and lower the lid.

3.Let cook for 4 full minutes.

4.Open the lid and crack the eggs onto the plate. Season with salt and pepper.

5.Add the bread slices to the plate, as well.

6.Cook for 4 minutes, turning the bread and bacon (and the eggs if you desire) over ha-lfway through.

7.Transfer carefully to a plate. Enjoy!

Nutritional Value:

- Calories 434
- Total Fats 19.6g
- Carbs 38.8g
- Protein 25.6g
- Fiber: 6g

EARLY MORNING BREAKFAST BRUSCHETTA

There's nothing like waking up to the taste of a great breakfast bruschetta. A great way to start the day off right! This one is yummy!

Prep Time: 10 Minutes

Cook Time: 10 Minutes

Servings: 4-5

Ingredients:

French bread (sliced 1" thick)

3 Tbsp. unsalted butter, divided

4 large eggs

1/4 cup whole milk

1 Tbsp. chopped chives

1/8 tsp. fresh black pepper

3/4 cup mashed avocado

1 cup diced tomatoes

Directions:

• Brush 2 tablespoons of the melted butter.

• Brush both sides of each slice.

• Place the bread slices on panini press grill for 2 about minutes until toasted and set it aside.

• Whisk together the eggs, chives, milk and pepper in a medium bowl.

• Get a medium nonstick pan over medium-low heat and add the rest of the butter (1 tablespoon) in the pan.

• Pour the eggs in and scramble to your liking.

• Spread a small part of the mashed avocado on one side of each piece of the toast. Last...put the avocado with the scrambled eggs on top and garnish with the diced tomatoes.

16

SPICY BRUSCHETTA WITH DIJON

You would never think of putting a little Dijon on a piece of toasted bread to make a Bruschetta till now. This is freaking amazing and you have to try it to believe it. So here it is for you!

Prep Time: 10 Minutes

Cook Time: 3-5 Minutes

Servings: 4-6

Ingredients

1 baguette , cut in half long ways

2 tsp. minced garlic (jar is fine)

3 tbsp. extra-virgin olive oil

1/4 cup grated parmesan cheese

2 1/2 cups minced tomatoes (cut really fine till pasty)

1 tbsp. Dijon mustard

1/3 cup thinly sliced fresh basil leaf

2 tbsp. balsamic vinegar

1/2 tsp. salt

1 tsp. fresh ground pepper

Directions

• Add the tomatoes, garlic, basil, vinegar, olive oil, cheese, salt and pepper in a bowl or container.

- Mix up very good and let sit for at least 20 minutes at room temperature.
- The flavors will marinade over this time to blend together.
- Slice the bread into individual pieces and place the bread slices on panini press grill for 2 about minutes until toasted.
- Spoon the mixture on top of the toasted bread and enjoy.

17

BACON EGG AND SAUSAGE BREAKFAST PANINI

This Panini is perfect for all meat lovers. It's packed with so much flavor thanks to the meat, cheese, bell pepper, and pesto. It's so good you might want 2!

Prep Time: 20 Minutes

Cook Time: 6 Minutes

Servings: 2

Ingredients:

2 pita breads

1/2cup pesto

2 eggs

1 cup shredded sharp cheddar cheese

1 cup shredded Monterey Jack cheese

1 cup shredded mozzarella cheese

1 pork sausage patty, cooked

2 strips bacon, cooked

1/3 cup roasted red pepper

1-2 tbsps. butter, melted

2 scallions, chopped

Directions:

• Use a whisk to beat the egg with a pinch of salt and pepper.

Place the butter in a skillet and melt it on medium heat. Use a spoon to stir the eggs and push them across the pan. Cook until the eggs set, about 1 to 2 minutes.

• Chop the sausage into small pieces. Spread the pesto on half of both pieces of pita. Top the pitas with half the cheese, then eggs, bacon, sausage, bell pepper, the remaining, cheese and then top with the scallions. Fold the other side of the pita on top of the filling, and spread the butter on the outside of the pitas.

• Cook the Panini on medium heat for 4 to 6 minutes, flipping halfway through. The bread should be brown, and the cheese should be melted.

18

CULINARY CAPRESE BRUSCHETTA

This part-perfect appetizer will have your friends asking for this wonderful recipe that will be the hit at any party for friends or family.

Prep Time: 10 Minutes

Cook Time: 5 Minutes

Servings: 6-8

Ingredients:

8 ounces of balsamic vinegar

8 ounces of fresh Mozzarella

2 tbsp. fresh chopped basil

2 cups cherry tomatoes

1 French baguette loaf

Directions:

• Heat the balsamic vinegar into a small pan or skillet.

• You will heat this oil at low/medium temperature. You will know when it is ready when it slowly comes to a light boil.

• Let it simmer…about 6-8 minutes. Then the vinegar will start thickening while it is cooking. As it is cooking the amount in the pan will shrink to about half, when it does this, cut off the heat.

- Pour all of the vinegar into a container to cool off. It will thicken the more it cools and will be more like a glaze.
- Take the mozzarella and chop it up.
- Cut the tomatoes in thirds.
- Chop the basil into strips and mix the tomatoes, mozzarella and basil.
- Slice the baguette into desired slice size. 1-2" thick. If you want to toast then put the slices down on the panini press and cover with butter or olive oil. Cook for 1-2 minutes until golden brown.
- Serve with the bruschetta on top of the baguette and a balsamic glaze drizzle on top.

19

THE ULTIMATE BACON BRUSCHETTA

Did I hear someone just say ??? If you guessed bacon... then you are correct! Bacon goes well on literally anything and these delightful and tasty treats may have you making this one for an entire week!

Prep Time: 10 Minutes

Cook Time: 3-5 Minutes

Servings: 4-6

Ingredients

6 bacon strips, chopped

4 ciabatta rolls

2 tbsp. olive oil

2 medium tomatoes, seeded and chopped

1/4 tsp. salt

1/8 tsp. pepper

3/4 cup crumbled feta cheese

16 fresh basil leaves, thinly sliced

1/2 cup balsamic vinaigrette

Directions

• Cook bacon over medium heat until crisp in a pan or skillet. You can also cook the bacon in your Panini press if desired.

- Drain the bacon on a paper towel of some sort.
- Cut rolls in half, then cut each half into quarters.
- Brush both sides of the bread with oil.
- Place the bread slices on panini press grill for 2 about minutes until toasted.
- Mix the tomatoes, salt and pepper in a bowl of some kind.
- Put on top of each piece of toasted bread the tomato mixture, cheese, basil bacon and drizzle with vinaigrette.
- Serve immediately while toast is still warm.

20

CHOCOLATE HAZELNUT FRENCH TOAST PANINI

This Panini has a beautiful flavor profile. The richness of the chocolate hazelnut spread provides some richness to the sweetness of the French toast, and the hazelnuts provide a perfect crunch in contrast to the soft inside of the French toast!

Prep Time: 20 Minutes

Cook Time: 6 Minutes

Servings: 4

Ingredients:

6 large eggs

1 cup whole milk

1/2 cup heavy cream

1/4 cup fresh orange juice (from about 1 medium orange)

2 tbsps. vanilla extract

2 tbsps. cognac (optional)

2 tbsps. granulated sugar

1/2 tsp ground cinnamon

Pinch of freshly grated nutmeg

Salt

8 slices Texas toast or other thick white bread

½ cup hazelnut spread with coco a

¼ cup chopped hazelnuts, toasted
Confectioners' sugar, for garnish
Pure maple syrup, for garnish

Directions:

• Spread the hazelnut spread on 4 of the pieces of bread and then place the hazelnuts on top. Top with the pieces of bread.

• Use a whisk to combine the eggs, milk, cream, orange juice, cognac, sugar, cinnamon, and vanilla. Put the sandwiches in a shallow baking dishes and cover with the mixture you just created. Allow the sandwiches to rest in the mixture for 10 min.

• Preheat your flip sandwich maker on medium high heat.

• Cook the Panini for 6 to 7 minutes in your preheated flap sandwiched maker, flipping halfway through.

• Top with confectioners' sugar and maple syrup

21

FRESH GARLIC TOMATO BRUSCHETTA

Nothing beats the taste of fresh tomato and garlic as a combination and powerful punch on the taste buds. This is one of those "Grab em' before they're gone" kind of dish!

Prep Time: 10 Minutes

Cook Time: 3-5 Minutes

Servings: 4-6

Ingredients

1/2 pound ripe tomatoes, at room temperature (3 to 4 medium)

Salt and fresh ground black pepper, to taste

2 tbsp. extra virgin olive oil

6 basil leaves, thinly sliced

Six 1/2-inch thick slices Italian or French bread

2 cloves garlic, peeled and left whole

• Take tomatoes and half them, removing and discarding most of the seeds.

• Cut tomatoes into medium chunks, then adding them to a medium bowl. Add salt, black pepper, to taste, basil and one tablespoon of olive oil. Stir and let sit several minutes to marinade the flavors together.

• Spread the rest of the oil on the bread slices.

• Place the bread slices on panini press grill for 2 about minutes until toasted and set it aside.

• Spread garlic on one side of the bread while it is still warm.

• Stir the tomato mix again to see if it needs added seasoning. Spoon a nice helping on each slice. Spread some of the juice that is left at the bottom of the bowl on top of the tomatoes.

22

PANCETTA CHERRY TOMATO AND EGG ENGLISH MUFFIN PANINI

This Panini features a variety of flavors. Pancetta is like an Italian form of bacon, the cherry tomatoes give it sweetness, and the mozzarella gives it creaminess.

Prep Time: 15 Minutes

Cook Time: 6 Minutes

Servings: 1

Ingredients:

1 English muffin

1 egg

5 cherry tomatoes

Fresh basil, chopped

2 slices of mozzarella

Olive oil

1 tsp butter

4 thin slices of pancetta, cooked

Directions:

• Use a whisk to beat the egg with a pinch of salt and pepper. Place the butter in a skillet and melt it on medium heat. Use a spoon to stir the eggs and push them across the pan. Cook until the eggs set, about 1 to 2 minutes.

• Put a layer of avocado on the Harissa side of the 2 pieces of bread, then the sausage, then the arugula, and top with the cheese. Then place the other two pieces of bread on top of the cheese. Brush the top and bottom of the sandwiches with olive oil.

• Cook the Panini on medium heat for 4 to 6 minutes, flipping halfway through. The bread should be toasted, and the cheese should be melted.

23

PROSCIUTTO AND EGG BAGEL PANINI

This Panini is great for breakfast sandwich and bagel lovers. The prosciutto adds a nice saltiness to the cheese, and the rich flavor of the eggs. Use your favorite bagel to make it special!

Prep Time: 10 Minutes

Cook Time: 3 Minutes

Servings: 2

Ingredients:

2 eggs

2 everything bagels (or any favorite bagel)

2 tbsps. mayonnaise

2 slices American cheese

4 slices prosciutto

2 handfuls baby arugula

Kosher salt

Ground black pepper

Olive oil

2 tsp butter

Directions:

• Use a whisk to beat the egg with a pinch of salt and pepper. Place the butter in a skillet and melt it on medium heat. Use a spoon to stir the eggs and push them across the pan. Cook until the eggs set, about 1 to 20 minutes.

• Cut the bagels in half horizontally. Spread the mayonnaise on the inside of the bagel. Layer the eggs, on the inside of 2 of the bagel halves, then the cheese, then the arugula, then the prosciutto. Top with the remaining pieces of bagel. Brush the top and bottom of the sandwiches with olive oil.

• Cook the Panini on medium heat for 2 to 3 minutes, flipping halfway through. The bagels should be toasted, and the cheese should be melted.

24

PARMESAN CHEESE-N-PEAS BRUSCHETTA

Like mom used to tell you…"Eat your peas!!!" So, we brought this dish to you from an inspired chef who used to have this said to them frequently when they were younger. You will love this dish as much as we did! Enjoy!

Prep Time: 5 Minutes

Cook Time: 5 Minutes

Servings: 4-5

Ingredients

12 slices of baguette bread

1/2 garlic clove

1 cup peas (thawed fresh or froze),

Kosher salt

2 tbsp.-virgin olive oil

Shaved Parmesan

Torn mint

A few drops of balsamic vinegar

Directions

• Place the bread slices on panini press grill for 2 about minutes until toasted.

• Then rub the toast with the garlic clove to coat.

• Blanch peas in a medium pan of boiling salted water till they turn a little tender.

• Drain the peas and move them to a bowl and sprinkle with sea salt and virgin olive oil. Mash the peas with back of a fork.

• Use a tablespoon and spread mixture on the toasted bread. Top with Parmesan cheese, mint, and just a hint of balsamic vinegar.

25

SPICY CHOCOLATE HAZELNUT BACON FRENCH TOAST PANINI

So many delicious layers of flavor here. Delicious nuttiness from the chocolate hazelnut spread, heat from the cayenne, and bacon. Yumm!

Prep Time: 20 Minutes

Cook Time: 6 Minutes

Servings: 4

Ingredients:

6 large eggs

1 cup whole milk

1/2 cup heavy cream

1/4 cup fresh orange juice (from about 1 medium orange)

2 tbsps. vanilla extract

2 tbsps. cognac (optional)

2 tbsps. granulated sugar

1/2 tsp ground cinnamon

Pinch of freshly grated nutmeg

Pinch of salt

Cayenne Pepper

8 strips of bacon, cooked

8 slices Texas toast or other thick white bread

½ cup hazelnut spread with coco a

¼ cup chopped hazelnuts, toasted

Confectioners' sugar, for garnish

Pure maple syrup, for garnish

Directions:

• Spread the hazelnut spread on 4 of the pieces of bread and then place the bacon on top. Add cayenne pepper to taste. Top with the pieces of bread.

• Use a whisk to combine the eggs, milk, cream, orange juice, cognac, sugar, cinnamon, and vanilla. Put the sandwiches in a shallow baking dishes and cover with the mixture you just created. Allow the sandwiches to rest in the mixture for 10 min..

• Preheat your flip sandwich maker on medium high heat.

• Cook the Panini for 6 to 7 minutes in your preheated flap sandwiched maker, flipping halfway through.

• Top with confectioners' sugar and maple syrup

BEEF AND PORK RECIPES

26

CHIPOTLE BBQ RIBS

Preparation Time: 5 minutes
Cooking Time: 16 minutes
Servings: 4
Ingredients:
•1-pound Back Ribs
•3 tbsp Brown Sugar
•1 ¾ cups BBQ Sauce
•2/3 cups Balsamic Vinegar
•½ tsp Chipotle Pepper
•¼ tsp Garlic Powder
•Salt and Pepper, to taste
Method:
1.Preheat your grill to 325 degrees F.
2.Sprinkle the ribs with salt, pepper, and garlic powder, and place on the bottom plate of the grill.
3.Cook for 8 minutes with the lid lowered.
4.In the meantime, combine the balsamic, BBQ sauce, sugar, and chipotle.
5.Lift the lid and sprinkle the mixture over the ribs.

6.Cook uncovered for about 8 more minutes, occasionally flipping over and adding more sauce as needed.

7.Serve and enjoy!

Nutritional Value:

•Calories 400

•Total Fats 9g

•Carbs 75g

•Protein 7g

•Fiber: 1g

27

SPICY BEEFY & HORSERADISH CHEESE PANINI

This will hit the spot for any meat lover. The horseradish and jalapeno give this sandwich some nice heat that's balanced perfectly by the cheese

Prep Time: 20 Minutes

Cook Time: 6 Minutes

Servings: 4

Ingredients:

1/3 cup mayonnaise

1/4 cup crumbled blue cheese

2 tsps. prepared horseradish

1/8 tsp pepper

1 large sweet onion, thinly sliced

1 tbsp. olive oil

8 slices white bread

8 slices provolone cheese

8 slices deli roast beef

2 tbsps. butter, softened

12 small jalapeno slices

Directions:

- Combine the mayonnaise, blue cheese, horseradish and pepper in a bowl.
- Sauté the onions in a skillet on medium heat until they become tender.
- Spread the bleu cheese mixture on a single side of each piece of bread.
- Place a layer of cheese, then jalapenos, beef, onions and then a second layer of cheese on half the pieces of bread. Place the other slices of bread on top.
- Butter the top and bottom of the sandwich and cook the Panini on medium heat for 6 minutes, flipping halfway through. The bread should be brown, and the cheese should be melted.

CLASSIC PATTY MELT PANINI

This is a classic diner favorite. The rye bread, and onions give this sandwich loads of flavor.

Prep Time: 25 Minutes

Cook Time: 4 Minutes

Servings: 4

Ingredients:

2 tbsps. unsalted butter

1 large Vidalia or other sweet onion, sliced

1 lb. lean ground beef

1 tbsp. Worcestershire sauce

1/2 tsp garlic powder

1/2 tsp dried oregano

1/4 tsp black pepper

8 slices seedless rye

1/4 lb. thinly sliced reduced-fat American cheese, about 8 slices

1/4 cup light Thousand Island salad dressing

Directions:

• Melt the butter in a large skillet on medium heat. Add the onions and cook for about 20 minutes. While the onions are

cooking combine the beef, Worcestershire sauce, and the seasoning. Form the beef into patties that are similar in shape to the bread. Place the patties in the skillet with the onions for the last 5 minutes of cooking. Flip the meat once halfway through

• Put a slice of cheese on a piece of bread then a patty, the onions and top with another slice of cheese and top with another piece of bread. Repeat the process with the remaining sandwiches.

• Cook the sandwiches for 4 minutes on medium heat, and make sure to flip halfway through. The bread should be brown, and the cheese should be melted. Serve the sandwiches with a side of the Thousand Island dressing.

29

ROASTED GARLIC MAYONNAISE AND LAMB PANINI WITH THYME

The beautiful flavor of the lamb is highlighted in this sandwich. The roasted garlic adds a sweet flavor that pairs well with the thyme and mayonnaise.

Prep Time: 10 Minutes

Cook Time: 55 Minutes

Servings: 4

Ingredients:

12 thin slices boneless, roasted leg of lamb

2 heads garlic

1/2 cup mayonnaise

2 tbsps. lemon juice

1 tbsp. fresh thyme leaves

Salt and freshly ground black pepper

4 paper-thin slices sweet onion

Fresh spinach leaves

1 large tomato, thinly sliced

4 soft sandwich rolls

Olive oil

Directions:

• Preheat your oven to 375F. Than use a knife to cut off the heard of the garlic cloves. Cut about ¼ inch from the top. The idea is to expose the inside of every garlic clove, and then drizzle with the oil. Bake for 45 to 50 minutes. The garlic should be sweet and soft. Allow the garlic to cool until you can handle it. Then separate the cloves from the bulb. Mash the cloves in a bowl.

• Mix the lemon juice, mayonnaise, and thyme with the mashed garlic until well combined. Allow it to rest for 15 minutes.

• Cut the sandwich rolls in half and spread the garlic mixture on the inside part of both halves of the rolls. Brush the other side of the bread with olive oil. Put a layer of onions on the bottom half of the roll, then tomatoes, spinach, and then lamb, and top with the other half of the roll.

• Cook the sandwiches for 5 minutes on medium heat, and make sure to flip halfway through. The bread should be nicely toasted.

30

LAMB AND HAVARTI GRILLED CHEESE PANINI

Your lamb leftovers are calling for this easy sandwich. The Havarti adds delicious creamy balance to the lamb and the spinach gives it a nice crunch.

Prep Time: 10 Minutes
Cook Time: 8 Minutes
Servings: 1

Ingredients:

2 slices thick hearty bread
1 tbsp. butter, room temperature
1/2 cup Havarti, shredded
1/4 cup leftover lamb, reheated
sliced red onion
handful of spinach
2 tbsps. tzatziki, room temperature

Directions:

• Spread butter on one side of each piece of bread.

• Place a layer of cheese down, then the lamb, spinach onions, and tzatziki on one piece of bread. Make sure it's not on the buttered side. Then top with the other piece of bread, making sure the buttered side is up.

• Cook the sandwiches 8 minutes on medium heat, and make sure to flip halfway through. The bread should be brown, and the cheese should be melted.

31

GARLICKY MARINATED STEAK

Preparation Time: 2 minutes

Cooking Time: 8 minutes

Servings: 1

Ingredients:

•4 Steaks (about 1 - 1 ½ pounds)

•3 tbsp minced Garlic

•¼ cup Soy Sauce

•2 tbsp Honey

•¼ cup Balsamic Vinegar

•2 tbsp Worcesteshire Sauce

•½ tsp Onion Powder

•Salt and Pepper, to taste

Method:

1.Whisk together the garlic, sauces, and spices, in a bowl.

2.Add the steaks to it and make sure to coat them well.

3.Cover with plastic foil and refrigerate for about an hour.

4.Preheat your grill to high.

5.Open and add your steaks to the bottom plate.

6.Lower the lid and cook for about 4 minutes, or until the meat reaches the internal temperature that you prefer.

7.Serve as desired and let sit for a couple of minutes before enjoying!

Nutritional Value:

- Calories 435
- Total Fats 24g
- Carbs 19g
- Protein 37g
- Fiber: 1g

32

HAWAIAN KEBOBS

Preparation Time: 70 minutes
Cooking Time: 6 minutes
Servings: 4
Ingredients:
- ½ cup Orange Juice
- 1 tbsp minced Garlic
- 1/3 cup Brown Sugar
- ½ tbs minced Ginger
- ½ cup Soy Sauce
- 1-pound Top Sirloin
- 1-pound Pineapple, fresh
- 2 Bell Peppers
- ½ Red Onion

Method:
1.Place the first 5 ingredients in a medium bowl. Whisk to combine well.

2.Cut the steak into pieces and add to the bowl.

3.Stir well to coat, cover with plastic wrap, and place in the fridge for at least 60 minutes.

4.Meanwhile, cut the red onion, pineapple, and bell pepper, into chunks.

5.If using wooden skewers, soak them in cold water.

6.Preheat your grill to medium-high.

7.Thread the steak, pineapple, onion, and bell peppers onto the skewers.

8.Open the grill and arrange the skewers onto the bottom plate.

9.Cover, and let cook for 6 minutes.

10. Serve and enjoy!

Nutritional Value:

•Calories 460

•Total Fats 13g

•Carbs 51g

•Protein 33g

•Fiber: 0.7g

33

BACON CHEDDAR AND TOMATO PANINI

This melty Panini will have you drooling. The flavors of bacon, cheddar, and tomato, combine to create a delicious all American flavor.

Prep Time: 15 Minutes
Cook Time: 7 Minutes
Servings: 4

Ingredients:

4 Roma tomatoes, halved lengthwise, pulp and seeds removed
olive oil
coarse sea salt
fresh ground black pepper
8 basil leaves, thinly sliced
2 tbsps. unsalted butter, melted
8 slices sourdough bread
8 slices bacon, fully cooked
4 ounces sharp cheddar cheese, thinly sliced

Directions:

• Preheat a small skillet on high heat.

• Use a brush to coat the cut side of the tomatoes with olive oil and salt and pepper to taste. Put the tomatoes on the skillet with the cut side down. Allow them to cook for 10 to 12 minutes. The tomatoes. Flip the tomatoes about halfway through. The tomatoes should be wrinkly and the tomatoes should be soft to the touch. Check the tomatoes constantly throughout the process so they don't overcook. Once cooked take them out of the skillet and season with basil.

• Spread the butter on one side of each piece of bread. Place 2 pieces of bacon on the unbuttered side of a piece of bread, then 2 tomatoes and a ¼ of the cheese. Then top with the other piece of bread making sure the butter side is on top.

• Cook the Panini on medium heat for 5-7 minutes, flipping halfway through. The bread should be brown, and the cheese should be melted.

34

CLASSIC PATTY MELT PANINI

This is a classic diner favorite. The rye bread, and onions give this sandwich loads of flavor.

Prep Time: 25 Minutes

Cook Time: 4 Minutes

Servings: 4

Ingredients:

2 tbsps. unsalted butter

1 large Vidalia or other sweet onion, sliced

1 lb. lean ground beef

1 tbsp. Worcestershire sauce

1/2 tsp garlic powder

1/2 tsp dried oregano

1/4 tsp black pepper

8 slices seedless rye

1/4 lb. thinly sliced reduced-fat American cheese, about 8 slices

1/4 cup light Thousand Island salad dressing

Directions:

• Melt the butter in a large skillet on medium heat. Add the onions and cook for about 20 minutes. While the onions are

cooking combine the beef, Worcestershire sauce, and the seasoning. Form the beef into patties that are similar in shape to the bread. Place the patties in the skillet with the onions for the last 5 minutes of cooking. Flip the meat once halfway through

• Put a slice of cheese on a piece of bread then a patty, the onions and top with another slice of cheese and top with another piece of bread. Repeat the process with the remaining sandwiches.

• Cook the sandwiches for 4 minutes on medium heat, and make sure to flip halfway through. The bread should be brown, and the cheese should be melted. Serve the sandwiches with a side of the Thousand Island dressing.

35

BACON MOZZARELLA, ZUCCHINI AND TOMATO PANINI

This is a delicious twist on the BLT. You use grilled Zucchini instead of lettuce, and add in creamy mozzarella for a heavenly sandwich.

Prep Time: 10 Minutes
Cook Time: 8 Minutes
Servings: 4

Ingredients:

6 slices bacon
1/2 large zucchini, cut lengthwise into 1/4" slices and grilled
3 tbsp. extra-virgin olive oil, divided
kosher salt
Freshly ground black pepper
1 medium yellow tomato, thinly sliced
1 medium red tomato, thinly sliced
1 loaf Ciabatta, halved lengthwise
8 oz. mozzarella, thinly sliced
2 tbsp. Freshly Chopped Basil

Directions:

• Put the tomatoes on a plate lined with paper towel in order to soak up any excess liquid.

• Use a brush to coat the inside of the bread with olive oil. Put down a layer of zucchini, then bacon, basil, and finally tomatoes. Salt and pepper to taste and top with top piece of bread. Use a brush to coat the top and bottom of sandwich.

• Spread the butter on one side of each piece of bread. Place 2 pieces of bacon on the unbuttered side of a piece of bread, then 2 tomatoes and a $\frac{1}{4}$ of the cheese. Then top with another piece of bread making sure the butter side is on top.

• Cook the Panini on medium high heat for 6 to 8 minutes, flipping halfway through. The bread should be brown, and the cheese should be melted.

SPICY SOPPRESSATA PANINI WITH PESTO AND MOZZARELLA

This spicy Italian salami has a great flavor. The mozzarella adds creaminess and the pesto gives a nice herbal flavor.

Prep Time: 15 Minutes

Cook Time: 10 Minutes

Servings: 4

Ingredients:

1 Ciabatta loaf, cut into 4 portions, or 4 Ciabatta rolls

1/2 cup basil pesto, purchased or homemade

8 ounces fresh mozzarella cheese, sliced

4 ounces sliced spicy Soppressata salami

Directions:

• Cut the Ciabatta in half horizontally.

• Spread the pesto on the inside of each piece of bread. Place a layer of salami on the bottom piece of bread and then place the cheese on top. Top with the other piece of bread

• Cook the Panini on medium high heat for 5 to 7 minutes, flipping halfway through. The bread should be brown, and the cheese should be melted.

BÁNH MÌ PANINI

A Bánh Mì a sandwich is a delicious sandwich from Vietnam. It combines delicious French flavors with some Vietnamese flare thanks to the jalapeno and pickled vegetables.

Prep Time: 10 Minutes

Cook Time: 4 Minutes

Servings: 1

Ingredients:

1 petite baguette roll or 7-inch section from a regular baguette

Mayonnaise

Maggi Seasoning sauce or light (regular) soy sauce

Liver pâté, boldly flavored cooked pork, sliced and at room temperature

3 or 4 thin, seeded cucumber strips, preferably English

2 or 3 sprigs cilantro, coarsely chopped

3 or 4 thin slices jalapeno chili

1/4 cup Daikon and Carrot Pickle

Directions:

• Cut the bread in half lengthwise. Use your fingers to take out some of the soft part of the middle of both pieces of bread.

• Spread the mayonnaise inside both pieces of bread. Lightly coat with the Maggi seasoning sauce, then place the meat on top followed by the cucumbers, cilantro, jalapenos, and then pickles.

• Cook the Panini on medium heat for 4 minutes, flipping halfway through. The bread should be nicely toasted.

38

BABBA GHANOUSH AND FETA LAMB PANINI

This is a great way to use leftover lamb. The beautiful Mediterranean flavors hit the spot, and the grilled pita or flatbread is delicious.

Prep Time: 20 Minutes
Cook Time: 6 Minutes
Servings: 4

Ingredients:

1 cup canned grilled eggplant pulp
1 small clove garlic, coarsely chopped
1 tbsp. tahini (sesame paste)
1/2 medium lemon
Salt
Freshly ground black pepper
2 to 3 sprigs flat-leaf parsley, chopped
8 to 12 ounces roasted leg of lamb
4 oval pita breads or flatbreads, cut in half horizontally
1 to 2 tbsps. olive oil
3/4 cup crumbled feta cheese

Directions:

• Place the eggplant, garlic, 1 tsp lemon juice, and tahini in a food processor. Pulse the mixture until it becomes smooth, and then salt and pepper to taste.

• Slice the lamb into bite sized piece. If you use pita bread use a brush to lightly coat both sides with olive oil. If you're using flatbread just coat one side.

• Spread the babba ghanoush spread on one side of the bread. If you're using flatbread make sure it's not the side with olive oil. Put the lamb on top of the babba ghanoush, then top with the feta, and finally sprinkle with the parsley. Top with another piece of pita or flatbread. Make sure the oil side is up if you're using flatbread

• Cook the sandwiches for 4 to 6 minutes on medium heat, and make sure to flip halfway through.

39

MOZZARELLA AND PESTO BEEF PANINI

This is filled will lots of classic Italian flavor. The pesto provides an aromatic flavor that pairs well with the creaminess of the mozzarella, and the rich flavor of beef.

Prep Time: 15 Minutes

Cook Time: 5 Minutes

Servings: 4

Ingredients:

8 slices Italian bread, 1/2 inch thick

2 tbsps. butter or margarine, softened

1/2 cup basil pesto

1/2 lb. thinly sliced cooked deli roast beef

4 slices (1 oz. each) mozzarella cheese

Marinara sauce, warmed, if desired

Directions:

• Spread the pesto on one side of each piece of bread. Spread the butter on the other side.

• Split the roast beef between four pieces of bread with the pesto side up and then top with the mozzarella. Place the other piece of bread on the mozzarella with the butter side up.

- Cook the Panini on medium heat for 5 minutes, flipping halfway through. The bread should be brown, and the cheese should be melted

40

PESTO PROSCIUTTO PANINI

This a great idea if you want a light dinner especially if you serve it with a salad. The saltiness of the prosciutto is balanced out by the fresh herbal flavor of the pesto.

Prep Time: 10 Minutes

Cook Time: 8 Minutes

Servings: 4

Ingredients:

One 10-ounce loaf Ciabatta, halved horizontally and soft interior removed

1/3 cup Pesto

Extra-virgin olive oil

1/3 lb. Prosciutto de Parma, thinly sliced

Tapenade (optional)

1/4 lb. Fontina cheese, thinly sliced

1/2 cup baby arugula or basil, optional

Coarse salt and fresh ground pepper

Directions:

• Spread pesto on one of the interior sides and olive oil on the other.

• Put in a layer of prosciutto, then arugula or basil, then

cheese. Top it off with a light drizzle of olive oil and a sprinkle of salt and pepper. Top with the other piece of bread.

• Brush the inside each piece of bread with the dressing. Then top the bottom pieces of bread with cheese. Add the mortadella, salami, tomatoes and pepperoncini's

• Cook the Panini on medium-high heat for 8 minutes, flipping halfway through. The bread should be brown, and the cheese should be melted.

41

PROSCIUTTO AND FIG PANINI

This is a delicious and simple Italian Panini. The saltiness of the prosciutto is balanced out by the sweetness of the figs, and pepperiness of the arugula.

Prep Time: 10 Minutes

Cook Time: 6 Minutes

Servings: 4

Ingredients:

8 (0.9-ounce) slices crusty Chicago-style Italian bread

4 ounces very thinly sliced prosciutto

1 1/4 cups (4 ounces) shredded Fontina cheese

1/2 cup baby arugula leaves

1/4 cup fig preserves

Olive oil

Directions:

• Lightly coat the one side of each piece of bread with olive oil using a brush.

• Spread the fig preserve on 4 pieces of bread (not on the olive oil side). On the other pieces of bread put a layer of prosciutto, then arugula and top with cheese. Place the fig coated bread on top with the fig side touching the cheese.

• Cook the Panini on medium heat for 6 minutes, flipping halfway through. The bread should be brown, and the cheese should be melted.

42

MUFFULETTA PANINI

This sandwich is a classic from the food capital of New Orleans. The olive salad on top and the 3 different types of pork cold cuts make this sandwich unique.

Prep Time: 10 Minutes

Cook Time: 4 Minutes

Servings: 4

Ingredients:

softened butter

8 slices rustic bread or 8 slices sourdough bread

16 slices provolone cheese (thin slices) or 16 slices mozzarella cheese (thin slices)

1/2 cup olive salad, drained or 1/2 cup olive tapenade

6 ounces thinly sliced black forest ham

6 ounces sliced mortadella

4 ounces sliced genoa salami

Directions:

• Spread butter on both sides of each piece of bread.

• Place 2 pieces of cheese on 4 pieces of bread. Then put down a layer of olive salad, ham, mortadella, salami and top with the remaining cheese. Then top with another piece of bread

• Cook the Panini on medium heat for 4 minutes, flipping halfway through. The bread should be brown, and the cheese should be melted.

43

CABBAGE AND CORNED BEEF PANINI

This is a perfect way to combine these two favorites. The Muenster makes for a tasty texture contrast to the corned beef and cabbage.

Prep Time: 20 Minutes

Cook Time: 8 Minutes

Servings: 2

Ingredients:

1 cup thinly sliced green cabbage

1 tbsps. olive oil

¼ tsp. table salt

Freshly ground black pepper

1 tsp. yellow mustard seeds

2 tbsps. unsalted butter, softened

4 1/2-inch-thick slices rye bread with caraway seeds

1 tbsps. grainy mustard, more to taste

12 thin slices (6 oz.) corned beef

6 thin slices (3 oz.) Muenster cheese

¼ cup water

Directions:

• Mix the water, cabbage, olive oil, mustard seeds, salt, and pepper in a saucepan, heat on medium-high heat until water boils. Once boiling lower heat to medium-low heat, cover, allow the mixture to cook for 10 to 15 minutes, stirring every once in a while. Remove the cabbage from the saucepan, and set aside any remaining water in the pan.

• Butter one side of each piece of bread and place mustard on the other side. Top two pieces of bread, mustard side up with corned beef, then cabbage, and finally cheese. Top with the remaining pieces of bread, butter side up.

• Cook the sandwiches for 6 to 8 minutes on medium heat, and make sure to flip halfway through. The bread should be brown, and the cheese should be melted.

44

STEAK SKEWERS WITH POTATOES AND MUSHROOMS

Preparation Time: 35 minutes
   Cooking Time: 10 minutes
   Servings: 6
   Ingredients:
   •1-pound Steak
   •4 tbsp Olive Oil
   •½ pound Button Mushrooms
   •4 tbsp Balsamic Vinegar
   •1 pound Very Small Potatoes, boiled
   •2 tsp minced Garlic
   •½ tsp dired Sage
   •Salt and Pepper, to taste
   Method:
   1.Start by cutting the steak into 1-inch pieces.
   2.Quarter the mushrooms.
   3.Whisk the vinegar, oil, garlic, sage, and salt and pepper, in a
bowl.
   4.Add the meat, murshooms and potatoes to the bowl, coat
well, and place in the fridge for 30 minutes. If your potatoes are

not small enough for the skewers, you can chop them into smaller chunks.

5.In the meantime, soak the skewers in cold water.

6.Meanwhile, preheat your grill to medium-high.

7.Thread the chunks onto the skewers and arrange them on the bottom plate.

8.Keep the lid open and cook for 5.

9.Flip over and cook for 5 more minutes.

10. Serve and enjoy!

Nutritional Value:
•Calories 383
•Total Fats 23g
•Carbs 21g
•Protein 23g
•Fiber: 3g

45

SALAMI AND TALEGGIO PANINI WITH SPICY FENNEL HONEY

This sandwich is so easy to make but delicious. The lovely flavor of the fennel permeates the spicy honey and adds complexity to the salty flavor of the salami.

Prep Time: 10 Minutes

Cook Time: 10 Minutes

Servings: 6

Ingredients:

1/3 cup honey

1 tbsp. fennel seeds

2 tsps. chili flakes

1/2 loaf focaccia, cut into 4-inch squares

1 lb. Taleggio, rind washed, room temperature, thinly sliced

12 slices fennel salami, thinly sliced

Directions:

• Put the chili, fennel, and honey in a small saucepan and heat on medium heat. Allow the mixture to cook for 3 to 5 minutes.

• Cut the focaccia in half horizontally. Layer the cheese on one piece of bread and layer the salami on top. Top the salami with a nice drizzle of the honey. Put the other piece of bread on top.

• Brush the inside each piece of bread with the dressing. Then top the bottom pieces of bread with cheese. Add the mortadella, salami, tomatoes and pepperoncini's

• Cook the Panini on medium-high heat for 10 minutes, flipping halfway through. The bread should be brown, and the cheese should be melted.

• Top with more honey and serve warm.

46

MINT CHILI CHUTNEY WITH LAMB PANINI

The lamb gets kicked up a notch in this sandwich. The mint gives it a fresh flavor, and the caramelized onions gives a sweetness that mixes well with the heat of the chutney.

Prep Time: 20 Minutes

Cook Time: 55 Minutes

Servings: 4

Ingredients:

¾ cup Chili Chutney

2 tsp fresh mint, finely chopped

1 tsp wholegrain mustard

2 tbsps. sour cream or cream cheese

Salt and freshly ground black pepper

4 Panini rolls or olive Ciabatta rolls, cut in half

4-8 slices roast lamb

½ cup caramelized red onion

½ cup feta cheese, crumbled

1½ cup arugula

Directions:

• Combine the chutney, mint, mustard, sour cream, and pepper. Allow it to rest for 15 minutes

• Spread the chutney mixture on the inside part of both halves of the rolls. Brush the other side of the bread with olive oil. Put a layer of onions on the bottom half of the roll, then lamb, arugula, and then feta, and top with the other half of the roll.

• Cook the sandwiches for 6 minutes on medium heat, and make sure to flip halfway through. The bread should be nicely toasted and the cheese should be melted.

47

LAMB AND HAVARTI GRILLED CHEESE PANINI

Your lamb leftovers are calling for this easy sandwich. The Havarti adds delicious creamy balance to the lamb and the spinach gives it a nice crunch.

Prep Time: 10 Minutes
Cook Time: 8 Minutes
Servings: 1

Ingredients:

2 slices thick hearty bread
1 tbsp. butter, room temperature
1/2 cup Havarti, shredded
1/4 cup leftover lamb, reheated
sliced red onion
handful of spinach
2 tbsps. tzatziki, room temperature

Directions:

• Spread butter on one side of each piece of bread.

• Place a layer of cheese down, then the lamb, spinach onions, and tzatziki on one piece of bread. Make sure it's not on the buttered side. Then top with the other piece of bread, making sure the buttered side is up.

• Cook the sandwiches 8 minutes on medium heat, and make sure to flip halfway through. The bread should be brown, and the cheese should be melted.

48

LAVISH LAMB PANINI BURGER

The lamb gets a lovely flavor from all the spices. The bread gets nice and crispy thanks to juices and fat released from the lamb as it cooks.

Prep Time: 10 Minutes

Cook Time: 10 Minutes

Servings: 8

Ingredients:

2 1/2 lbs. ground lamb, preferably shoulder

1 medium onion, very finely chopped

3/4 cup chopped fresh flat-leaf parsley

1 tbsp. ground coriander

3/4 tsp ground cumin

1/2 tsp ground cinnamon

2 tsps. kosher salt

1 1/2 tsps. freshly ground black pepper

1/4 cup olive oil, plus more for grilling

8 thick medium pita breads with pockets

Directions:

• Combine the lamb, oil, and seasoning using a fork. Allow the meat to rest, covered for an hour.

• Open up the pitas and fill them with the lamb mixture. Use the fill the seal the pita.

• Cook the sandwiches for 10 minutes on medium heat, and make sure to flip halfway through. The bread should be nicely crunchy and the lamb is cooked through.

49

MOZZARELLA AND PESTO BEEF PANINI

This is filled will lots of classic Italian flavor. The pesto provides an aromatic flavor that pairs well with the creaminess of the mozzarella, and the rich flavor of beef.

Prep Time: 15 Minutes

Cook Time: 5 Minutes

Servings: 4

Ingredients:

8 slices Italian bread, 1/2 inch thick

2 tbsps. butter or margarine, softened

1/2 cup basil pesto

1/2 lb. thinly sliced cooked deli roast beef

4 slices (1 oz. each) mozzarella cheese

Marinara sauce, warmed, if desired

Directions:

• Spread the pesto on one side of each piece of bread. Spread the butter on the other side.

• Split the roast beef between four pieces of bread with the pesto side up and then top with the mozzarella. Place the other piece of bread on the mozzarella with the butter side up.

• Cook the Panini on medium heat for 5 minutes, flipping halfway through. The bread should be brown, and the cheese should be melted

50

BUFFALO MELT PATTY PANINI

These are perfect for game day. The give this sandwich a lovely kick that's balanced perfectly by the cheese

Prep Time: 25 Minutes

Cook Time: 4 Minutes

Servings: 4

Ingredients:

2 tbsps. unsalted butter

1 large Vidalia or other sweet onion, sliced

1 lb. lean ground beef

1 tbsp. Worcestershire sauce

1/2 tsp garlic powder

1/4 tsp black pepper

8 slices seedless rye

1/4 lb. thinly sliced Swiss cheese, about 8 slices

1/4 cup blue cheese dressing

1 cup mayonnaise

1 cup buffalo hot sauce

Directions:

• Melt the butter in a large skillet on medium heat. Add the onions and cook for about 20 minutes. While the onions are

cooking combine the beef, Worcestershire sauce, and the seasoning. Form the beef into patties that are similar in shape to the bread. Place the patties in the skillet with the onions for the last 5 minutes of cooking. Flip the meat once halfway through.

- Mix the buffalo sauce and mayonnaise in a medium bowl.
- Spread the buffalo sauce mixture on one side of each piece of bread.
- Put a slice of cheese on a piece of bread then a patty, the onions and top with another slice of cheese and top with another piece of bread. Repeat the process with the remaining sandwiches.
- Cook the sandwiches for 4 minutes on medium heat, and make sure to flip halfway through. The bread should be brown, and the cheese should be melted. Serve the sandwiches with a side of the blue cheese dressing.

51

PORK BURNT ENDS

Preparation Time: 10 minutes

Cooking Time: 6 minutes

Servings: 1

Ingredients:

• 1-pound Pork Shoulder

• 2 tbsp Favorite Rub Spice

• 2 tbsp Honey

• 1 ½ tbsp Barbecue Sauce

Method:

1. Start by chopping the pork into cubes.

2. Place the meat in a bowl and add the spice, honey, and barbecue sauce.

3. With your hands, mix wel, making sure that each meat cube gets a little bit of honey, sauce, and spices.

4. Preheat your grill to 375 degrees F.

5. Arange the pork onto the bottom plate and lower the lid.

6. Cook for about 6 minutes.

7. Check the meat – if it is not too burnt for your taste, cook for an additional minute.

8. Serve as desired.

9.Enjoy!

Nutritional Value:

•Calories 399

•Total Fats 27g

•Carbs 10.8g

•Protein 27g

•Fiber: 0g

52

BABBA GHANOUSH AND FETA LAMB PANINI

This is a great way to use leftover lamb. The beautiful Mediterranean flavors hit the spot, and the grilled pita or flatbread is delicious.

Prep Time: 20 Minutes

Cook Time: 6 Minutes

Servings: 4

Ingredients:

1 cup canned grilled eggplant pulp

1 small clove garlic, coarsely chopped

1 tbsp. tahini

(sesame paste)

1/2 medium lemon

Salt

Freshly ground black pepper

2 to 3 sprigs flat-leaf parsley, chopped

8 to 12 ounces roasted leg of lamb

4 oval pita breads or flatbreads, cut in half horizontally

1 to 2 tbsps. olive oil

3/4 cup crumbled feta cheese

Directions:

• Place the eggplant, garlic, 1 tsp lemon juice, and tahini in a food processor. Pulse the mixture until it becomes smooth, and then salt and pepper to taste.

• Slice the lamb into bite sized piece. If you use pita bread use a brush to lightly coat both sides with olive oil. If you're using flat-bread just coat one side.

• Spread the Babba Ghanoush spread on one side of the bread. If you're using flatbread make sure it's not the side with olive oil. Put the lamb on top of the Babba Ghanoush, then top with the feta, and finally sprinkle with the parsley. Top with another piece of pita or flatbread. Make sure the oil side is up if you're using flatbread

• Cook the sandwiches for 4 to 6 minutes on medium heat, and make sure to flip halfway through.

SWEET AND SALTY BACON CHEESY PANINI

This will satisfy your sweet and salt craving all at once. The bacon adds some delicious saltiness to the sweetness of the apple butter.

Prep Time: 10 Minutes

Cook Time: 3 Minutes

Servings: 4

Ingredients:

8 oz. Brie, thinly sliced

8 pieces thick cut bacon, fully cooked

8 pieces Raisin-walnut bread

$\frac{1}{2}$ cup Apple butter

Butter, softene d

Directions:

• Spread the apple butter on one side of each piece of bread. Then add 2 pieces of bacon to apple butter side of one piece of bread and top with $\frac{1}{4}$ of the cheese. Place another piece of bread on top with the apple butter side of the bread touching the cheese. Spread butter on the other side of both pieces of bread.

• Cook the Panini on medium high heat for 2-3 minutes, flipping halfway through. The bread should be brown when ready.

MAPLE PORK CHOPS

Preparation Time: 65 minutes

Cooking Time: 7-8 minutes

Servings: 1

Ingredients:

•4 boneless Pork Chops

•6 tbsp Balsamic Vinegar

•6 tbsp Maple Syrup

•¼ tsp ground Sage

•Salt and Pepper, to taste

Method:

1.Whisk the vinegar, maple, sage, and some salt and pepper in a bowl.

2.Add the pork chops and coat well.

3.Cover with plastic foil and refrigerate for one hour.

4.Preheat your grill to 350 degrees F.

5.Open and arrange the chops onto the bottom plate.

6.Lower the lid and cook closed for about 7 minutes, or until your desired doneness is reached.

7.Serve and enjoy!

Nutritional Value:

- Calories 509
- Total Fats 19g
- Carbs 15g
- Protein 65g
- Fiber: 0g

55

BUFFALO MELT PATTY PANINI

These are perfect for game day. The give this sandwich a lovely kick that's balanced perfectly by the cheese

Prep Time: 25 Minutes

Cook Time: 4 Minutes

Servings: 4

Ingredients:

2 tbsps. unsalted butter

1 large Vidalia or other sweet onion, sliced

1 lb. lean ground beef

1 tbsp. Worcestershire sauce

1/2 tsp garlic powder

1/4 tsp black pepper

8 slices seedless rye

1/4 lb. thinly sliced Swiss cheese, about 8 slices

1/4 cup blue cheese dressing

1 cup mayonnaise

1 cup buffalo hot sauce

Directions:

• Melt the butter in a large skillet on medium heat. Add the onions and cook for about 20 minutes. While the onions are cooking combine the beef, Worcestershire sauce, and the seasoning. Form the beef into patties that are similar in shape to the bread. Place the patties in the skillet with the onions for the last 5 minutes of cooking. Flip the meat once halfway through.

• Mix the buffalo sauce and mayonnaise in a medium bowl.

• Spread the buffalo sauce mixture on one side of each piece of bread.

• Put a slice of cheese on a piece of bread then a patty, the onions and top with another slice of cheese and top with another piece of bread. Repeat the process with the remaining sandwiches.

• Cook the sandwiches for 4 minutes on medium heat, and make sure to flip halfway through. The bread should be brown, and the cheese should be melted. Serve the sandwiches with a side of the blue cheese dressing.

56

HERBED LEMONY PORK SKEWERS

Preparation Time: 10 minutes

Cooking Time: 8 minutes

Servings: 4

Ingredients:

• 1-pound Pork Shoulder or Neck

• 1 tsp dried Basil

• 1 tsp dried Parsley

• 1 tsp dried Oregano

• 2 Garlic Cloves, minced

• 4 tbsp Lemon Juice

• ¼ tsp Onion Powder

• Salt and Pepper, to taste

Method:

1. Start by soaking 8 skewers in cold water, to prevent the wood from burning on the grill.

2. Cut the pork into small chunks and place in a bowl.

3. Add lemon juice, garlic, spices and herbs to the bowl.

4. Give the mixture a good stir so that the meat is coated well.

5. Preheat your grill to medium-high.

6. Meanwhile, thread the meat onto the skewers.

7.When the green light turns on, arrange the skewers onto the bottom plate.

8.Cook for about 4 minutes per side (or more if you like the meat well-done and almost burnt).

9.Serve as desired and enjoy!

Nutritional Value:

•Calories 364

•Total Fats 27g

•Carbs 1.6g

•Protein 26.7g

•Fiber: 0.1g

57

ITALIAN COLD CUT CLASSIC PANINI

This just like the hoagies you get at an Italian deli. All the flavors meld together so well when they're heated up in and cheese is melted.

Prep Time: 10 Minutes

Cook Time: 6 Minutes

Servings: 2

Ingredients:

1 12 inch hoagie rolls or the bread of your choice

1 tbsp. olive oil

2 ounces Italian dressing

4 slices provolone cheese

4 slices mortadella

8 slices genoa salami

8 slices deli pepperoni

4 slices tomatoes

2 pepperoncini peppers, chopped

Directions:

• Slice the rolls in half and then cut it open.

• Lightly coat the outside of the roll with olive oil using a brush.

• Brush the inside each piece of bread with the dressing. Then top the bottom pieces of bread with cheese. Add the mortadella, salami, tomatoes and pepperoncini's

• Cook the Panini on medium heat for 6 minutes, flipping halfway through. The bread should be brown, and the cheese should be melted.

POULTRY RECIPES

58

SPINACH AND PESTO CHICKEN PANINI

This is a delicious light and fresh sandwich. The spinach gives the sandwich a nice crunch, the pesto gives a jolt of flavor and cheese provides some gooey creaminess.

Prep Time: 10 Minutes

Cook Time: 5 Minutes

Servings: 1

Ingredients:

1/2 cup mayonnaise

2 tbsps. prepared pesto

1 1/2 cups shredded rotisserie chicken

Kosher salt

Freshly ground pepper

1 1lb. Ciabatta loaf, split lengthwise and cut into 4 pieces

Extra-virgin olive oil, for brushing

1 cup lightly packed baby spinach

8 thin slices of Swiss chees e

Directions:

• Use a whisk to combine the pesto and mayonnaise. Then mix in the chicken and salt and pepper to taste.

• Use a brush to coat the top and bottom of the bread with

olive oil. Put a layer of chicken on the bottom piece of bread, then spinach, and finally cheese. Place the top piece of bread on the cheese.

• Cook the sandwiches for 7 minutes on medium heat, and make sure to flip halfway through. The bread should be brown, and the cheese should be melted.

59

BUFFALO CHICKEN PANINI

This Panini is an easy way to get your buffalo wings fix. The onions give a little bit of sweetness and the cheese helps to balance out spice from the buffalo sauce.

Prep Time: 30 Minutes

Cook Time: 4 Minutes

Servings: 4

Ingredients:

2 cups shredded cooked chicken

1 large sweet onion, sliced

8 slices seedless rye

1/4 lb. thinly sliced Swiss cheese, about 8 slices

1/4 cup blue cheese dressing

1 cup mayonnaise

1 cup buffalo hot sauce

2 tbsps. unsalted butter

blue cheese dressing

Directions:

• Melt the butter in a large skillet on medium heat. Add the onions and cook for about 20 minutes.

- Mix the buffalo sauce and mayonnaise in a medium bowl and toss with the chicken.
- Put a slice of cheese on a piece of bread then the chicken, the onions and top with another slice of cheese and top with another piece of bread. Repeat the process with the remaining sandwiches. Spread the butter on the top and bottom of the sandwich
- Cook the sandwiches for 4 minutes on medium heat, and make sure to flip halfway through. The bread should be brown, and the cheese should be melted. Serve the sandwiches with a side of the blue cheese dressing.

60

CHICKEN YAKITORI

Preparation Time: 70 minutes

Cooking Time: 6 minutes

Servings: 4

Ingredients:

•2 tbsp Honey

•1 tsp minced Garlic

•1-pound boneless Chicken

•1 tsp minced Ginger

•4 tbsp Soy Sauce

•Salt and Pepper, to taste

Method:

1.In a bowl, combine the honey, ginger, soy sauce, and garlic. Add some salt and pepper.

2.Cut the chicken into thick stripes and add them to the bowl.

3.Mix until the meat is completely coated with the marinade.

4.Cover the bowl and refrigerate for about one hour.

5.Preheat your grill to medium.

6.Thread the chicken onto metal (or soaked wooden) skewers and arrange onto the bottom plate.

7.Lower the lid and cook for about 6-7 minutes, depending on how well-cooked you prefer the meat to be.

8.Serve and enjoy!

Nutritional Value:

•Calories 182
•Total Fats 9g
•Carbs 10g
•Protein 27g
•Fiber: 0.2g

61

DIJON AND BERRY CHICKEN PANINI

This has a beautiful mix of sweet and spicy. The blackberries pair so well with the mustard, and peppery flavor of the arugula.

Prep Time: 16 Minutes

Cook Time: 6 Minutes

Servings: 4

Ingredients:

4 Bakery Ciabatta rolls or French hamburger buns

2 tbsps. herb garlic butter, melted

1/3 cup fresh blackberries (about 6 berries)

1 tbsp. honey

1/2 cup stone-ground mustard

3.5 oz. Deli aged white cheddar cheese, shredded

1 medium red onion, coarsely chopped

1 cup fresh baby arugula, coarsely chopped

1 Deli rotisserie chicken, shredded

Directions:

• Slice the rolls in half horizontally. Mash the berries in a bowl, and mix with the honey and then mix in the mustard. In a separate bowl mix together the chicken, arugula, cheese, and onions.

• Spread butter on the outside of the bread. Spread the berry mixture on the inside of the bread. Put chicken mixture on the inside of the bottom piece of bread, and place the top piece of bread on the chicken.

• Cook the sandwiches for 6 minutes on medium heat, and make sure to flip halfway through. The bread should be brown, and the cheese should be melted.

62

CHICKEN PORTOBELLO PANINI

This is a delicious and simple Panini. The Portobello adds a lovely earthiness to chicken, and the tomatoes add some freshness.

Prep Time: 15 Minutes

Cook Time: 6 Minutes

Servings: 4

Ingredients:

1 tbsp. olive oil

1 tbsp. red wine vinegar

1/2 tsp Italian Seasoning Mix

1/2 tsp salt

1/4 tsp coarsely ground black pepper

1 garlic clove, pressed

2 large Portobello mushroom caps

2 slices (1/2 inch thick) large white onion

1 cup (4 ounces) grated Provolone cheese

2 plum tomatoes, sliced

8 slices (3/4 inch thick) Italian bread

1 cup shredded roasted chicken

Directions:

• Preheat a skillet on medium heat for 5 minutes. Then place the onions and the mushrooms in the skillet. Allow them to cook for about 4 to 6 minutes, making sure to flip halfway through. Cut the onions in half and the mushrooms into thin slices.

• Brush what's going to be the outside of the bread with olive oil. Top half the pieces of bread with a layer cheese, then, chicken, then mushrooms, then onions, then tomatoes, and a second layer of cheese. Top with another piece of bread making sure the olive oil side is on the outside.

• Cook the sandwiches for 6 minutes on medium heat, and make sure to flip halfway through. The bread should be brown, and the cheese should be melted.

63

BRUSCHETTA TURKEY PANINI

This is a great way to get all the flavor of bruschetta in sandwich form. The turkey's light flavor allows, the basil, tomatoes, and mozzarella to shine.

Prep Time: 10 Minutes
Cook Time: 4 Minutes
Servings: 4

Ingredients:

8 slices Italian bread
8 fresh basil leaves
8 thinly sliced tomatoes
16 slices of Black Pepper Turkey Breast
4 pieces of mozzarella cheese
4 tbsps. mayonnaise
Olive oil

Directions:

• Cut the basil into ribbons.

• Place a layer of turkey on a piece of bread, then basil, and then cheese. Spread the mayo on the bottom part of the top piece of bread, and place it on top of the cheese. Brush the top and bottom of the sandwich with olive oil

- Cook the sandwiches for 4 minutes on medium heat, and make sure to flip halfway through. The bread should be brown, and the cheese should be melted.

64

BASIL GRILLED CHICKEN WITH ASPARAGUS

Preparation Time: 15 minutes

Cooking Time: 7 minutes

Servings: 4

Ingredients:

- 1 tsp Dijon Mustard
- 1 pound boneless and skinless Chicken Breasts
- 1 tsp dried Basil
- 1 tsp minced Garlic
- 2 tbsp Olive Oil
- ¼ tsp Onion Powder
- 12 Asparagus Spears
- Salt and Pepper, to taste

Method:

1. Combine the oil, mustard, basil, garlic, onion powder, and some salt and pepper, in a bowl.

2. Coat the chicken with this mixture.

3. Meanwhile, preheat your grill to 350 degrees F.

4. Arrange the chicken breasts onto the bottom plate.

5. Season the asparagus with salt and pepper and add them next to the chicken.

6.Lower the lid, and cook closed, for 7 full minutes, or until your preferred doneness is reached.

7.Serve and enjoy!

Nutritional Value:

•Calories 350

•Total Fats 24g

•Carbs 6g

•Protein 26g

•Fiber: 2g

65

WHISKEY WINGS

Preparation Time: 10 minutes

Cooking Time: 6 minutes

Servings: 4

Ingredients:

- 1 tbsp Whiskey
- 1/2 tbsp Chili Powder
- 1 tsp Paprika
- 20 Chicken Wings
- ¼ tsp Garlic Powder
- Salt and Pepper, to taste
- 2 tsp Brown Sugar

Method:

1. Preheat your grill to 375 degrees F.

2. In the meantime, dump all of the ingredients in a large bowl.

3. With your hands, mix well, to coat the chicken wings completely.

4. When the green light is on, open the grill and arrange the chicken wings onto it.

5. Lower the lid and cook closed for 6 minutes. You can check

near the end to see if you need to increase (or decrease) the grilling time for your preferred doneness.

6.Serve with rice and enjoy!

Nutritional Value:

•Calories 210

•Total Fats 21g

•Carbs 9.3g

•Protein 18g

•Fiber: 0g

66

BACON CHIPOTLE CHICKEN PANINI

This has everything you need for a heavenly sandwich. The sourdough has a little tartness, the bacon gives it some saltiness, the cheese gives it creaminess, and the chipotle gives it some spice.

Prep Time: 10 Minutes

Cook Time: 5 Minutes

Servings: 1

Ingredients:

2 slices sourdough bread

1/4 cup Caesar salad dressing

1 cooked chicken breast, diced

1/2 cup shredded Cheddar cheese

1 tbsp. bacon bits

1 1/2 tsps. chipotle chili powder, or to taste

2 tbsps. softened butte r

Directions:

• Spread the salad dressing on one side of both pieces of bread. Then top the dressing side of one piece of bread with chicken, then cheese, then bacon, and finally chipotle chili powder. Place the other piece of bread with the dressing side down on top. Butter the other side of both pieces of bread.

- Cook the Panini on medium heat for 5 minutes, flipping halfway through. The bread should be brown, and the cheese should be melted.

67

SIMPLE CAJUN CHICKEN LEGS

Preparation Time: 2 minutes

Cooking Time: 8 minutes

Servings: 1

Ingredients:

•8 Chicken Legs, boneless

•2 tbsp Olive Oil

•2 tbsp Cajun Seasoning

Method:

1.Preheat your grill to medium-high.

2.Brush them with the olive oil, and then rub the legs with the seasoning.

3.When the green light is on, arrange the legs onto the bottom plate.

4.Lower the lid, and let the legs cook closed, for about 8 to 10 minutes.

5.Serve with the favorite side dish, Enjoy!

Nutritional Value:

•Calories 370

•Total Fats 19.2g

- Carbs 0.5g
- Protein 35g
- Fiber: 0g

68

DUCK VEGGIE KEBOBS

Preparation Time: 15 minutes

Cooking Time: 7 minutes

Servings: 2

Ingredients:

•8 ounces boneless and skinless Duck (breast is fine)

•1/2 small Squash

•½ Zucchini

•1 small Red Bell Pepper

•¼ Red Onion

•2 tbsp Olive Oil

•1 tbsp Balsamic Vinegar

•2 tsp Dijon Mustard

•2 tsp Honey

•Salt and Pepper, to taste

Method:

1.Whisk together the oil, vinegar, mustard, honey, and some salt and pepper, in a bowl.

2.Cut the duck into chunks and dump into the bowl.

3.Mix to coat well and set aside. You can leave in the fridge for an hour or two, but if you are in a hurry, you can place on the grill straight away – it will taste great, as well.

4.Cut the veggies into chunks.

5.Plug the grill in, and set the temperature to 375 degrees F.

6.Thread the duck and veggies onto metallic skewers.

7.Open the grill and place on the bottom plate.

8.Lower the lid and cook for 5-8 minutes, depending on how done you want the meat to be.

9.Serve and enjoy!

Nutritional Value:

•Calories 250

•Total Fats 10g

•Carbs 11g

•Protein 30g

•Fiber: 2g

69

SOUTHWESTERN TURKEY PANINI

This sandwich is packed will all sorts of southwestern flavor. The chipotle mayo gives it a kick, the avocado gives it creaminess, and the Colby jack cheese gives it a depth of flavor.

Prep Time: 15 Minutes

Cook Time: 4 Minutes

Servings: 2

Ingredients:

1 medium Avocado peeled and seeded

½ tbsp. Cilantro leaves finely chopped

½ tsp Lime juice

Salt to taste

Chipotle mayonnaise (store bought or homemade)

4 slices large Sourdough bread

8 slices Colby Jack Cheese

8 slices Blackened Oven Roasted Turkey Breast

4 slices Tomato

Directions:

• Mash and mix the avocado, lime and cilantro, and then salt and pepper to taste.

• Spread the chipotle mayonnaise on one side of every piece

of bread. On 2 pieces of bread with the mayonnaise side facing up place a layer of cheese, then turkey, then tomato, then avocado mixture, then turkey, and finally cheese again. Top with another piece of bread with the mayonnaise side touching the cheese.

• Cook the sandwiches for 6 minutes on medium heat, and make sure to flip halfway through. The bread should be toasted, and the cheese should be melted.

70

SMOKED PROVOLONE AND TURKEY PANINI

This simple sandwich has a world of flavors in it. The provolone gives it a nice Smokey flavor which, works well with the spiciness of the Dijon, and the creaminess of the mayonnaise.

Prep Time: 5 Minutes

Cook Time: 10 Minutes

Servings: 4

Ingredients:

1 round Asiago Cheese Focaccia

3 tbsps. light mayonnaise

2 tsps. Dijon mustard

5 ounces thinly sliced smoked provolone

8 ounces thinly sliced smoked turkey breast

1 ripe beefsteak tomato, thinly sliced

1 ounce baby spinach leaves

Olive oil

Directions:

• Cut the bread in half horizontally.

• Spread a layer of mayonnaise and a layer of mustard on the inside of the top piece of bread. Place a layer of turkey on the inside of the bottom piece of bread then, spinach, then tomatoes, and top with cheese. Place the top piece of bread on the cheese with the mayonnaise side down. If necessary cut the sandwiches into wedges in order to fit it in your flip sandwich maker.

• Cook the sandwiches for 6 to 10 minutes on medium heat, and make sure to flip halfway through. The bread should be toasted, and the cheese should be melted. Cut the sandwiches into 4 wedges if you haven't already done so.

71

THE THANKSGIVING TURKEY CUBAN PANINI

This is another recipe that puts your thanksgiving leftovers to good use. This take on the famous Cuban sandwich adds cranberries to the Dijon mayonnaise and adds turkey to the traditional pork.

Prep Time: 15 Minutes

Cook Time: 7 Minutes

Servings: 4

Ingredients:

2 tbsps. mayonnaise

2 tbsps. Dijon mustard

2 tbsps. leftover cranberry sauce

Salt and freshly ground black pepper

4 slices good quality Italian bread

4 slices Swiss cheese

2 slices cooked ham

6 slices leftover cooked turkey

8 dill pickle slices

Olive oil

Directions:

• Mix together the first mayonnaise, cranberry sauce, and

Dijon mustard using a whisk. Salt and pepper to taste. Combine the mixture with the cabbage until well coated.

• Spread a layer of the newly made cranberry Dijon sauce on what's going to be the inside of 2 pieces of bread. Put a layer of cheese, then turkey, a layer of the ham, a layer of pickles, and another layer of cheese on the pieces of bread. Top with another piece of bread. Brush the top and bottom of the sandwich with olive oil

• Cook the sandwiches for 6 to 7 minutes on medium high heat, and make sure to flip halfway through. The bread should be toasted, and the cheese should be melted. Once you're ready to serve, slice the sandwiches in half.

72

THE ULTIMATE THANKSGIVING REUBEN PANINI

This is a great way to use your thanksgiving leftovers. The addition of cranberries to the Russian dressing makes this particular festive along with the substitution of turkey for corned beef.

Prep Time: 15 Minutes

Cook Time: 7 Minutes

Servings: 4

Ingredients:

1/3 cup mayonnaise

2 tbsps. cranberry sauce (I used whole berry)

2 tsps. freshly grated horseradish

1 tsp Worcestershire sauce

Kosher salt and black pepper, to taste

2 cups shredded green cabbage or packaged Cole slaw

8 slices rye bread

8 slices Swiss cheese

3/4 lb. carved turkey, thinly sliced

2 tbsps. melted butter

Directions:

• Mix together the first 4 ingredients using a whisk. Salt and pepper to taste. Combine the mixture with the cabbage until well coated.

- Put a layer of cheese, then turkey, a layer of the slaw, another layer of turkey, and another layer of cheese on a piece of bread. Top with another piece of bread. Spread the butter on the top and bottom of the sandwich
- Cook the sandwiches for 7 minutes on medium high heat, and make sure to flip halfway through. The bread should be toasted, and the cheese should be melted.

73

LEMON AND ROSEMARY TURKEY AND ZUCCHINI THREADS

Preparation Time: 70 minutes
Cooking Time: 7 minutes
Servings: 4

Ingredients:
- 1-pound Turkey Breasts, boneless and skinless
- 1 Large Zuchinni
- 2 tbsp Lemon Juice
- ½ tsp Lemon Zest
- ¼ cup Olive Oil
- 1 tbsp Honey
- 1 tbsp Fresh Rosemary
- ¼ tsp Garlic Powder
- Salt and Pepper, to taste

Method:
1. Cut the Turkey into smaller chunks, and place inside a bowl.
2. Add the olive oil, lemon juice, zest, honey, rosemary, garlic powder, and some salt and pepper, to the bowl.
3. With your hands, mix well until the turkey is completely coated with the mixture.
4. Cover and let sit in the fridge for about an hour.

5.Wash the zucchini thoroughly and cut into small chunks. Season with salt and pepper.

6.Preheat your Grill to 350 – 375 degrees F.

7.Thread the turkey and zucchini onto soaked (or metal) skewers and arrange on the bottom plate.

8.Lower the lid and cook closed for 6-7 minutes.

9.Serve and enjoy!

Nutritional Value:

•Calories 280

•Total Fats 23g

•Carbs 6g

•Protein 27g

•Fiber: 0.5g

74

TERIYAKI CHICKEN THIGHS

Preparation Time: 70 minutes
Cooking Time: 7 minutes
Servings: 4
Ingredients:
•4 Chicken Thighs
•½ cup Brown Sugar
•½ cup Teriyaki Sauce
•2 tbsp Rice Vinegar
•1 thumb-sized piece of Ginger, minced
•¼ cup Water
•2 tsp minced Garlic
•1 tbsp Cornstarch
Method:
1.Place the sugar, teriyaki sauce, vinegar, ginger, water, and garlic, in a bowl.
2.Mix to combine well.
3.Transfer half of the mixture to a saucepan and set aside.
4.Add the chicken thighs to the bowl, and coat well.
5.Cover the bowl with wrap, and place in the fridge. Let sit for one hour.

6.Preheat your grill to medium.

7.In the meantime, place the saucepan over medium heat and add the cornstarch. Cook until thickened. Remove from heat and set aside.

8.Arrange the thighs onto the preheated bottom and close the lid.

9.Cook for 5 minutes, then open, brush the thickened sauce over, and cover again.

10. Cook for additional minute or two.

11. Serve and enjoy!

Nutritional Value:

•Calories 321

•Total Fats 11g

•Carbs 28g

•Protein 31g

•Fiber: 1g

FISH & SEAFOOD RECIPES

75

LIME SEA BASS

Preparation Time: 5 minutes

Cooking Time: 9 minutes

Servings: 4

Ingredients:

•½ tsp Garlic Powder

•4 tbsp Lime Juice

•4 Sea Bass Fillets

•Salt and Pepper, to taste

Method:

1.Preheat your grill to 375 degrees F.

2.Brush the fillets with lime juice and sprinkle with garlic powder, salt, and pepper.

3.When the green light is on, open the grill, coat with cooking spray, and arrange the fillets on top.

4.Cook open for 4 minutes. Then flip over and cook for 4-5 more minutes on the other side.

5.Serve with rice or favorite side dish, ad enjoy!

Nutritional Value:

•Calories 130

- Total Fats 2.6g
- Carbs 0g
- Protein 24g
- Fiber: 0g

76

TUNA STEAK WITH AVOCADO & MANGO SALSA

Preparation Time: 10 minutes
    Cooking Time: 8 minutes
    Servings: 2
Ingredients:
•2 Tuna Steaks
•1 ½ tbsp Olive Oil
•1 tsp Paprika
•2 tbsp Coconut Sugar
•1 tsp Onion Powder
•¼ tsp Pepper
•½ tsp Salt
•2/3 tsp Cumin
Salsa:
•1 Avocado, pitted and diced
•1 Mango, diced
•1 tbsp Olive Oil
•1 tsp Honey
•½ Red Onion, diced
•2 tbsp Lime Juice
•Pinch of Salt

Method:

1.Preheat your grill to 350-375 degrees F.

2.Place the olive oil and spices in a small bowl and rub the tuna steaks with the mixture.

3.Place on top of the bottom plate and cook for 4 minutes.

4.Flip the steaks over and cook for another 4 minutes.

5.Meanwhile, prepare the salsa by placing all of the salsa ingredients in a bowl, and mixing well to combine.

6.Transfer the grilled tuna steaks to two serving plates and divide the avocado and mango salsa among them.

7.Enjoy!

Nutritional Value:

•Calories 280

•Total Fats 26g

•Carbs 12g

•Protein 24g

•Fiber: 2g

77

ORANGE-GLAZED SALMON

Preparation Time: 10 minutes
Cooking Time: 8 minutes
Servings: 4
Ingredients:
•4 Salmon Fillets
•½ tsp Garlic Powder
•1 tsp Paprika
•¼ tsp Cayenne Pepper
•1 ¾ tsp Salt
•1 tbsp Brown Sugar
•¼ tsp Black Pepper
Glaze:
•1 tsp Salt
•2 tbsp Soy Sauce
•Juice of 1 Orange
•4 tbsp Maple Syrup
Method:
1.Preheat your grill to medium and coat with cooking spray.
2.In a small bowl, combine the spices together, and then massage the mixture into the fish.

3.Arrange the salmon onto the bottom plate and cook with the lid off.

4.In the meantime, place the glaze ingredients in a saucepan over medium heat.

5.Cook for a couple of minutes, until thickened.

6.Once the salmon has been cooking for 3 minutes, flip it over.

7.Cook for another 3 minutes.

8.Then, brush with the glaze, lower the lid, and cook for an additional minute.

9.Serve with preferred side dish. Enjoy!

Nutritional Value:

•Calories 250

•Total Fats 19g

•Carbs 7g

•Protein 22g

•Fiber: 0g

78

THE EASIEST PESTO SHRIMP

Preparation Time: 20 minutes

Cooking Time: 5 minutes

Servings: 2

Ingredients:

• 1-pound Shrimp, tails and shells discarded

• ½ cup Pesto Sauce

Method:

1.Place the cleaned shrimp in a bowl and add the pesto sauce to it.

2.Mix gently with your hands, until each shrimp is coated with the sauce. Let sit for about 15 minutes.

3.In the meantime, preheat your grill to 350 degrees F.

4.Open the grill and arrange the shrimp onto the bottom plate.

5.Cook with the lid off for about 2-3 minutes. Flip over and cook for an additional 2 minutes.

6.Serve as desired and enjoy!

Nutritional Value:

• Calories 470

- •Total Fats 28.5g
- •Carbs 3g
- •Protein 50g
- •Fiber: 0g

79

BLACKENED TILAPIA

Preparation Time: 10 minutes

Cooking Time: 8 minutes

Servings: 4

Ingredients:

•4 Tilapia Fillets

•3 tsp Paprika

•½ tsp Garlic Powder

•¼ tsp Onion Powder

•¼ tsp Black Pepper

•¾ tsp Salt

•2 tbsp Olive Oil

Method:

1.Preheat your grill to 375 degrees F.

2.Place the oil and spices in a small bowl and mix to combine.

3.Rub the mixture into the tilapia fillets, making sure to coat well.

4.When the green light indicates the unit is ready for grilling, arrange the tilapia onto the bottom plate.

5.With the lid off, cook for 4 minutes.

6.Flip over, and thencook for another four minutes. Feel free to increase the cooking time if you like your fish especially burnt.

7.Serve as desired and enjoy!

Nutritional Value:

•Calories 175
•Total Fats 9g
•Carbs 1g
•Protein 23.5g
•Fiber: 0.6g

80

GRILLED SCALLOPS

Preparation Time: 10 minutes
Cooking Time: 6 minutes
Servings: 4
Ingredients:
•1-pound Jumbo Scallops
•1 ½ tbsp Olive Oil
•½ tsp Garlic Powder
•Salt and Pepper, to taste
Dressing:
•1 tbsp chopped Parsley
•3 tbsp Lemon Juice
•½ tsp Lemon Zest
•2 tbsp Olive Oil
•Salt and Pepper, to taste
Method:
1.Preheat your grill to medium-high.
2.Brush the scallops with olive oi, and sprinkle with salt, pepper, and garlic powder.
3.Arrange onto the bottom plate and cook for about 3 minutes, with the lid off.

4.Flip over, and grill for an additional two or three minutes.

5.Meanwhile, make the dressing by combining all of the ingredients in a small bowl.

6.Transfer the grilled scallops to a serving plate and drizzle the dressing over.

7.Enjoy!

Nutritional Value:

•Calories 102

•Total Fats 5g

•Carbs 3g

•Protein 9.5g

•Fiber: 1g

81

LEMON PEPPER SALMON WITH CHERRY TOMATOES AND ASPARAGUS

Preparation Time: 8 minutes

Cooking Time: 5 minutes

Servings: 4

Ingredients:

•4 Salmon Fillets

•8 Cherry Tomatoes

•12 Asparagus Spears

•2 tbsp Olive Oil

•½ tsp Garlic Powder

•1 tsp Lemon Pepper

•½ tsp Onion Powder

•Salt, to taste

Method:

1.Preheat your grill to 375 degrees F and cut the tomatoes in half.

2.Brush the salmon, tomatoes, and sparagus with olive oil, and then sprinkle with the spices.

3.Arrange the salmon fillets, cherry tomatoes, and asparagus spears, onto the bottom plate.

4.Gently, lower the lid, and cook the fish and veggies for about

5-6 minutes, or until you reach your desired doneness (check at the 5 th minute).

5.Serve and enjoy!

Nutritional Value:

•Calories 240

•Total Fats 14g

•Carbs 3.5g

•Protein 24g

•Fiber: 1.4g

VEGETARIAN & VEGGIE
RECIPES

82

PROVOLONE BABY MUSHROOM AND CARAMELIZED ONION PANINI

This Panini is the closest thing you're going to get to French onion soup in sandwich form. The caramelized onions are just like the onions found in French onion soup, and your bread mimics the delicious top of the soup. The mushrooms sop up all the delicious caramelized onion flavor and add a light earthiness.

Prep Time: 40 Minutes

Cook Time: 4 Minutes

Servings: 5

Ingredients:

2 tbsps. unsalted butter

2 tbsps. olive oil

1 and 1/2 large onions (or 2 medium) sliced into 1/4 inch thick slices

1 tbsp. sugar

1/4 tsp thyme

2 tbsps. minced garlic (I used 1 and 1/2)

1 tsp Worcestershire sauce

8 oz. fresh baby Bella mushrooms, sliced into 1/4 inch thick slices

1/2 tsp black pepper

salt to taste

1/4 - 1/2 tsp red pepper flakes (or more to taste)

1 tsp flour

1/4 cup mushroom broth (or beef broth)

2 tbsps. minced parsley

5 - 1 oz. slices provolone cheese, cut in half

10 slices of fresh French bread

Olive oil

Directions:

• Heat a big skillet on medium heat, making sure it's hot before adding any ingredients. Put in the olive oil and butter, and allow the butter to melt. Then put in the onions and allow them to cook for 5 minutes. Mix in the sugar and cook for an additional 15 minutes. Mix in the Worchester sauce, garlic, and thyme, and allow the mixture to cook for 2 more minutes before mixing in the mushrooms. Cook for 10 minutes before mixing in the red and black pepper along with the flour. Slowly mix in the broth 1 tbsp. at a time, waiting until it's been absorbed before adding another. After you've added all of the broth and it's been absorbed, remove it from the heat and mix in the parsley.

• Place a layer of cheese on 5 pieces of bread, then the vegetable mixture, and then another layer of cheese. Top with the remaining slices of bread. Brush the olive oil on both the top and bottom of the sandwiches.

• Cook the Panini on medium high heat for 3 to 4 minutes, flipping halfway through. The bread should be toasted, and the cheese should be melted.

83

THAI PEANUT PEACH PANINI WITH BASIL

This makes a delicious and unexpected dessert. The sweetness of the peaches is well paired by the creaminess of the peanut sauce, and the aromatic flavor of the basil.

Prep Time: 10 Minutes
Cook Time: 8 Minutes
Servings: 1

Ingredients:

2 tbsp. creamy natural peanut butter
1 tbsp. agave or maple syrup
1/2 tbsp. soy sauce or tamari
1/2 tbsp. lime juice
2 slices good sandwich bread
1 small or 1/2 large peach sliced thin
2 tbsp. fresh basil leaves
1-2 tsp. olive oil
Butter, softened

Directions:

• Mix together the first 4 ingredients using a whisk. If the sauce is too thick you can thin it out with a small amount of water. The sauce will natural thin when it's grilled.

• Spread a large amount of the peanut sauce on what's going to be the inside pieces of bread. Layer the peaches and basil on the peanut sauce side of one of the pieces of bread, and then top with the other. Spread the butter on the top and bottom of the sandwich

• Cook the Panini on medium heat for 6 to 8 minutes, flipping halfway through. The bread should be brown, and the cheese should be melted.

84

SHAVED ASPARAGUS AND BALSAMIC CHERRIES WITH PISTACHIOS PANINI

This Panini is a strange mix of flavor combinations. I'm sure you would never think to put cherries and asparagus together but they work.

Prep Time: 15 Minutes

Cook Time: 6 Minutes

Servings: 4

Ingredients:

1 to 1 and 1/2 cups pitted, chopped Bing cherries

zest from 2 lemons

3 to 4 tbsp. balsamic vinegar

roughly 1/2 bunch of thick-stalk asparagus, shaved with a mandolin or vegetable peeler

2 tbsp. fresh mint, thinly sliced

2 tbsp. fresh basil, thinly sliced

2 tbsp. pistachio oil

1 multigrain baguette, cut in half, and split open

ricotta

fresh mozzarella

salt and freshly-cracked pepper

1/2 tbsp. butter, softened

Directions:

• Mix the cherries, balsamic vinegar, and lemon zest. Then salt and pepper to taste.

• Mix the asparagus mint, pistachio oil, and basil in a separate bowl.

• Cut the mozzarella into slices that are 1/3 of an inch thick. Place them on the inside part of the pieces of bread and place the cherry mixture on top of it. Then place the asparagus mixture on top of that

• Use a knife top spread the ricotta on the inside of the top pieces of bread, and place it on the asparagus mixture.

• Cook the Panini on medium heat for 5 to 6 minutes, flipping halfway through. The bread should be brown, and the cheese should be melted.

• Cut the sandwiches in half before serving.

85

GOAT CHEESE & TOMATO STUFFED ZUCCHINI

Preparation Time: 2 minutes

Cooking Time: 8 minutes

Servings: 8

Ingredients:

•14 ounces Goat Cheese

•1 ½ cups Tomato Sauce

•4 medium Zucchini

Method:

1.Preheat your grill to medium-high.

2.Cut the zucchini in half and scoop the seeds out.

3.Coat the grill with cooking spray and add the zucchini to it.

4.Lower the lid and cook for 2 minutes.

5.Now, add half of the goat cheese first, top with tomato sauce, and place the remaining cheese on top. Place a piece of aluminum foil on top of the filling so you don't make a big mess.

6.Carefully lower the grill and cook for an additional minute.

7.Serve and enjoy!

Nutritional Value:

•Calories 170

- Total Fats 11g
- Carbs 8.2g
- Protein 10.5g
- Fiber: 2.3g

86

CAPRESE EGGPLANT BOATS

Preparation Time: 10 minutes

Cooking Time: 10 minutes

Servings: 4

Ingredients:

•2 Eggplants

•1 cup Cherry Tomatoes, halved

•1 cup Mozzarella Balls, chopped

•2 tbsp Olive Oil

•4 tbsp chopped Basil Leaves

•Salt and Pepper, to taste

Method:

1.Preheat your grill to 375 degrees F.

2.Cut the eggplants in half (no need to peel them- just wash well), drizzle with olive oil and season with salt and pepper, generously.

3.When the green light is on, open the grill and arrange the eggplant halves onto the bottom plate.

4.Lower the lid and cook for about 4-5 minutes, until well-done.

5.Transfer to a serving plate and top with cherry tomatoes, mozzarella and basil.

6.Serve and enjoy!

Nutritional Value:

•Calories 187

•Total Fats 11g

•Carbs 18.3g

•Protein 6.8g

•Fiber: 7.3g

87

RATATOUILLE PANINI

This is a take on the classic French dish. It makes for a delicious, healthy vegetarian sandwich that's perfect for lunch. The roasted red pepper sauce gives it a lot of flavor.

Prep Time: 30 Minutes

Cook Time: 16 Minutes

Servings: 1

Ingredients:

1 red bell pepper, sliced

1 tomato, chopped

1 clove garlic, minced

1 tsp dried oregano, or to taste

salt and ground black pepper to taste

1 eggplant, sliced

1 zucchini, sliced

1 tomato, sliced

1 red onion, sliced

4 tsps. olive oil

4 slices sourdough bread

4 slices mozzarella cheese

Directions:

• Warm a skillet on high heat, and place the red bell pepper in it for around 5 minutes. The pepper should be soft when it's ready. Place the red pepper, chopped tomato, garlic in a blender or food processor. Blend or process until a smooth sauce is formed. Add salt, pepper, and oregano to taste.

• Grill the remaining vegetable on a grille or the same skillet for about 6 minutes flipping halfway through. The vegetables will be soft when ready.

• Brush what's going to be the outside of the bread slices with olive oil. Spread the sauce on what's going to be the inside of the bread. Layer a piece of piece of cheese on 2 of the pieces of bread, then the vegetable mixture, then another piece of cheese. Top with another piece of bread with the sauce side touching the cheese.

• Cook the Panini on medium heat for 4 to 5 minutes, flipping halfway through. The bread should be toasted, and the cheese should be melted.

88

VEGAN PEPPER JACK ROASTED PEPPER PANINI

This spicy sandwich will hit the spot for any vegan. The peppers provide a world of flavor, the vegan cheese adds creaminess, and the Harissa adds some lovely heat.

Prep Time: 10 Minutes

Cook Time: 4 Minutes

Servings: 1

Ingredients:

2 slices bread (sourdough used)

2 tsp. vegan buttery spread

5 thin slices of tomato

1/4 cup (handful) of fresh basil leaves

1/4 - 1/3 cup vegan pepper jack cheese shreds such as Daiya

2-3 thin slices roasted red or yellow pepper

1/2 cup baby spinach

pinches of black pepper

1 tbsp. Harissa

Directions:

• Spread what's going to be the outside of each piece of bread with the vegan buttery spread. Spread the Harissas on what's going to be the inside of each piece of bread.

• Place the tomatoes on one of the pieces of bread, then the spinach, then the basil, then the peppers, and top with the vegan cheese. Place the other piece of bread on top with the Harissa touching the cheese.

• Cook the Panini on medium heat for 2 to 4 minutes, flipping halfway through. The bread should be brown, and the cheese should be melted.

89

LEMONY DELICIOUS SUMMER VEGETABLE PANINI

This Panini has all the bounty of summer, and a nice light lemony flavor. It's the perfect light summer lunch filled with vegetables and creamy ricotta cheese.

Prep Time: 15 Minutes

Cook Time: 4 Minutes

Servings: 4

Ingredients:

1 tbsps. olive oil

1 small onion, sliced

1 medium yellow squash, thinly sliced

1 medium zucchini, thinly sliced

1 red bell pepper, sliced

2 tsps. of lemon zest

$\frac{1}{4}$ tsp salt

4 Ciabatta rolls or 4 pieces of focaccia

1/8 tsp ground black pepper

1 cup part-skim ricotta cheese

2 tsps. lemon zest

1 $\frac{1}{2}$ tsps. lemon juice

1/8 tsp salt

1/8 tsp ground black pepper

Directions:

• Place the oil in a skillet and heat it on medium high heat. Cook the onions in the oil for about 3 to 4 seconds, until they start to soften. Mix in the squash, peppers and zucchini and cook for another 5 to 7 minutes. Mix in the first 2 tsps. of lemon zest and 1/8 tsp of pepper and the ¼ tsp of salt. Remove the mixture from the heat and set aside in a bowl.

• Mix the last 5 ingredients in a bowl.

• Slice the rolls in half horizontally and place a layer of the ricotta mixture on the inside of each piece of bread.

• Place the vegetable mixture on the bottom pieces of bread. Pot the top pieces of bread on the vegetables, making sure the ricotta side is touching the vegetables.

• Cook the Panini on medium high heat for 3 to 4 minutes, flipping halfway through. The bread should be brown, and the cheese should be melted.

90

PEACH CAPRESE PANINI

This is like having a delightful caprese salad with a sweet twist. The peach gives it a delightful sweetness that's balanced by the creamy mozzarella, the aromatic flavor of the basil, and the tartness of the balsamic vinegar. Try using burrata instead of mozzarella for even more creaminess

Prep Time: 10 Minutes

Cook Time: 4 Minutes

Servings: 1

Ingredients:

1 French deli roll, split

1 ½ tsp balsamic vinegar

2 slices mozzarella cheese

1 small heirloom tomato, sliced

4 fresh basil leaves

olive oil

1 small peach, sliced

Directions:

• Sprinkle the balsamic vinegar on the inside of both pieces of bread. Brush the outside of both pieces of bread with olive oil

• Place one of the mozzarella slices on the bottom piece of

bread, then the peaches, then the tomatoes, and top with the other piece of cheese. Place the other piece of bread on top of the cheese.

• Cook the Panini on medium heat for 3 to 4 minutes, flipping halfway through. The bread should be toasted, and the cheese should be melted.

91

GRILLED PIZZA MARGARITA

Preparation Time: 8 minutes

Cooking Time: 2 minutes

Servings: 1

Ingredients:

•1 Tortilla

•3 tbsp Tomato Sauce

•3 ounces shredded Mozzarella

•4 Basil Leaves, chopped

•Pinch of Salt

Method:

1.Preheat your grill to medium-high.

2.Unlock to lower the griddle and lay it on your counter.

3.When the green light turns on, add the tortilla to the grill, and lower the lid.

4.Cook only for about 40 seconds, just until it becomes hot.

5.Add the tomato sauce on top, sprinkle with cheese, basil, and some salt.

6.Cook for another minute or so − with the lid OFF − until the cheese becomes melted.

7.Serve and enjoy!

Nutritional Value:
- Calories 375
- Total Fats 22g
- Carbs 23g
- Protein 22g
- Fiber: 2g

92

HALOUMI KEBOBS

Preparation Time: 15 minutes

Cooking Time: 5 minutes

Servings: 4

Ingredients:

•½ pound Haloumi Cheese

•4 Cremini Mushrooms, cut in half

•1 Zucchini, cut into chunks

•½ Bell Pepper, cut into chunks

•2 tbsp Olive Oil

•Salt and Pepper, to taste

Method:

1.Preheat your grill to 375 degrees F.

2.Meanwhile, soak 8 wooden skewers in water to preven burning.

3.Cut the cheese int chunks.

4.Thread the cheese and veggies onto the skewers, drizzle with the olive oil and sprinkle with salt and pepper.

5.Arrange onto the bottom plate, lower the lid, and cook closed for about 5 minutes (or more if you want it well-done).

6.Serve as desired and enjoy!

Nutritional Value:
- Calories 220
- Total Fats 14g
- Carbs 6g
- Protein 5g
- Fiber: 1.2g

93

HUMMUS AND VEGETABLE PANINI

This Panini is incredibly easy to make, and so light and fresh. It's packed with wholesome vegetable, and delicious hummus.

Prep Time: 10 Minutes

Cook Time: 5 Minutes

Servings: 4

Ingredients:

1 tbsps. olive oil

1 small onion, sliced

1 medium zucchini, thinly sliced

1 medium cucumber, thinly sliced

1 red bell pepper, sliced

8 slices whole grain bread

4 tbsp. homemade or store-bought hummus of your choice

fresh spinach leaves

1 cup matchstick carrots

slice of provolone cheese

Directions:

• Spread the hummus on 1 side of 4 pieces of bread. Layer the vegetables starting with the zucchini, then, cucumber, then spinach then red bell pepper, then carrots. Top the vegetables with a slice of cheese and place another piece of bread on the cheese. Brush the top and bottom of the sandwich with olive oil

• Cook the Panini on medium heat for 4 to 5 minutes, flipping halfway through. The bread should be brown, and the cheese should be melted.

94

AVOCADO AND MIXED VEGETABLE PANINI

This Panini is so delicious and creamy thanks to the cheese and avocado. The sautéed vegetable is packed with flavor and all sorts of good vitamins and minerals.

Prep Time: 15 Minutes

Cook Time: 20 Minutes

Servings: 4

Ingredients:

1 1/2 tbsps. butter or olive oil

1 minced shallot (onion or garlic works too)

8 ounces sliced baby Portobello mushrooms

1 cup cherry or grape tomatoes

2 cups chopped kale, stems removed

salt to taste

2 avocados

8 pieces thick, sturdy wheat bread

White cheese like Provolone or Mozzarella

Olive oil

Directions:

• Put the butter in a big skillet and allow it to melt on medium heat. Put in the shallots and cook until they become translucent.

Mix in the mushrooms, and cook until they start to brown. Then mix in the kale and tomatoes, and cook until the kale wilts, and the tomatoes are cooked through.

• Mash the avocados using a fork. Spread the avocado on what's going to be the inside of each piece of bread. Then place a layer of cheese on half of the pieces of bread, then a layer of veggies, and finally another layer of cheese. Top with another piece of bread. Brush the top and bottom of the sandwich with olive oil

• Cook the Panini on medium heat for 4 to 5 minutes, flipping halfway through. The bread should be brown, and the cheese should be melted.

95

PAPRIKA & CHIPOTLE LIME CAULI-STEAKS

Preparation Time: 10 minutes

Cooking Time: 6 minutes

Servings: 4

Ingredients:

• 2 Cauliflower Heads

• 4 tbsp Olive Oil

• 1 tsp minced Garlic

• 1 tbsp Chipotle Powder

• 1 ½ tbsp Paprika

• 1 tsp Honey

• 1 tsp Salt

• Juice of 1 large Lime

• 1 tsp Lime Zest

Method:

1. Preheat your grill to medium-high.

2. Remove the outter leaves of the cauliflower and trim them well. Lay them flat onto your cutting board and then cut into steak-like pieces. (about 3 to 4 inches thick).

3. In a bowl, whisk together all of the remaining ingredients.

4.Brush the steaks with the mixture well, and then arrange them onto the bottom plate of the grill.

5.Lower the lid to cut the cooking time in half, and cook only for about 6 minutes, without turning over.

6.Transfer to a serving plate and enjoy!

Nutritional Value:

•Calories 202

•Total Fats 14g

•Carbs 16g

•Protein 6g

•Fiber: 8g

96

SPINACH AND CHEESE PORTOBELLOS

Preparation Time: 10 minutes

Cooking Time: 6 minutes

Servings: 3

Ingredients:

•3 Portobello Mushrooms

•2 cups Spinach, chopped

•1 cup shredded Cheddar Cheese

•4 ounces Cream Cheese

•1 tbsp Olive Oil

•1 tsp minced Garlic

•Salt and Pepper, to taste

Method:

1.Preheat your grill to 350 degrees F.

2.Clean the mushroom caps well, and pat dry with paper towels.

3.Remove the stems, so the filllign can fit.

4.Now, make the filling by mixing the cheeses, spinach, and garlic. Divide this mixture among the mushrooms.

5.Drizzle with olive oil.

6.When the green light is on, open the grill and add the mushrooms.

7.Arrange on top of the plate and cook with the lid off for about 5 minutes.

8.Now, lower the lid gently, but do not use pressure. Let cook for 15-20 seconds, just so the cheese melts faster.

9.Transfer to a serving plate and enjoy!

Nutritional Value:

•Calories 210

•Total Fats 9g

•Carbs 5g

•Protein 10g

•Fiber: 1g

97

CORN AND ZUCCHINI PEPPER JACK PANINI

This Panini is perfect for summer when you can get lots of zucchini and sweet corn. The pepper jack gives this sandwich some heat which is balanced out by the sweetness of the corn. The zucchini gives it a nice crunch

Prep Time: 10 Minutes

Cook Time: 10 Minutes

Servings: 4

Ingredients:

1 tbsp. olive oil

1 large clove garlic, minced

1 ear corn, kernels removed

1 small zucchini, quartered lengthwise and sliced

Salt + pepper to taste

8 slices bread

2 tbsp. butter, softened

1 cup shredded pepper jack cheese

Directions:

• Place the oil in a skillet and heat it on medium high heat. Cook the garlic in the oil for about 15 seconds, until it's fragrant. Mix in the corn and zucchini and cook for around 3 minutes. The zucchini should be soft but not mushy. Remove the mixture from the heat and salt and pepper to taste.

• Place a layer of cheese on 4 pieces of bread, then the vegetable mixture, and then another layer of cheese. Top with the remaining slices of bread. Butter both the top and bottom of the sandwich.

• Cook the Panini on high heat for 5 to 7 minutes, flipping halfway through. The bread should be brown, and the cheese should be melted.

98

GRILLED TOFU WITH PINEAPPLE

Preparation Time: 15 minutes
Cooking Time: 8 minutes
Servings: 4

Ingredients:
- 1 pound firm Tofu
- 1 Red Bell Pepper
- 1 Yello Bell Pepper
- 1 Zucchini
- ½ Pineapple
- ½ tsp Ginger Paste
- Salt and Pepper, to taste
- 2 tbsp Olive Oil

Method:
1. Preheat your grill to medium-high.
2. Meanwhile, chop the tofu and vegies into smaller chunks, and place in a bowl. If using wooden skewers, soak them into water before using.
3. Add ginger and oil to the bowl and mix until coated well.
4. Thread the veggies and tofu onto the skewers.

5.When the green light turns on, open the grill and arrange the skewers onto the bottom plate.

6.Cook for 4 minutes, then flip over and cook for additional four minutes.

7.Serve as desired and enjoy!

Nutritional Value:
•Calories 210
•Total Fats 12g
•Carbs 9g
•Protein 12g
•Fiber: 2g

SALAD RECIPES

99

SHRIMP SALAD WITH SOUR CREAM AND DIJON

Preparation Time: 10 minutes
  Cooking Time: 6 minutes
  Servings: 4
  Ingredients:
  •1-pound Shrimp
  •1 Lettuce Head
  •1 cup Baby Spinach
  •1 Cucumber
  •1 Tomato
  •1 tbsp chopped Parsley
  •½ cup Sour Cream
  •2 tbsp Lemon Juice
  •1 tbsp Honey
  •1 tbsp Dijon Mustard
  •2 tbsp Olive Oil
  •Salt and Pepper, to taste
  Method:
  1.Preheat your grill to medium-high.
  2.When the green light is on, grease with cooking spray.

3.Season the shrimp with salt and pepper and arrange onto the bottom plate.

4.Cook for 2-3 minutes, then flip over, and cook for 2-3 minutes more.

5.Meanwhile, chop the veggies and place in a large bowl.

6.When ready, transfer the shrimp to the bowl.

7.In another bowl, whisk together the remaining ingredients.

8.Drizzle the sour cream mixture over the salad.

9.Serve and enjoy!

Nutritional Value:

•Calories 245

•Total Fats 16g

•Carbs 12g

•Protein 20g

•Fiber: 2.2g

100

GRILLED WATERMELON SALAD WITH CUCUMBER AND CHEESE

Preparation Time: 10 minutes

Cooking Time: 4 minutes

Servings: 4

Ingredients:

•1 Small Watermelon (approximately yielding 4 cups when cubed)

•1 tbsp chopped Basil

•1 Cucumber, chopped

•3 ounces Feta Cheese, crumbled or cubed

•Juice of 1 Lime

•1 tbsp Olive Oil

•Salt and Pepper, to taste

Method:

1.Preheat your grill to medium.

2.Peel and slice the watermelon (discard any seeds).

3.Open the grill and arrange the watermelon onto the bottom plate.

4.Lower the lid and cook for 4 minutes.

5.Transfer to a cutting board and slice into chunks.

6.Place into a bowl and add the rest of the ingredients.

7.Toss well to combine and coat.

8.Serve and enjoy!

Nutritional Value:

•Calories 122

•Total Fats 5g

•Carbs 17g

•Protein 4g

•Fiber: 1g

101

GRILLED ZUCCHINI AND FETA SALAD

Preparation Time: 10 minutes

Cooking Time: 3 minutes

Servings: 4

Ingredients:

- 1 Large Zucchini
- 1 cup Baby Spinach
- ½ cup crumbled Feta Cheese
- 1 cup Cherry Tomatoes, cut in half
- 1 cup Corn
- 3 tbsp Olive Oil
- 1 tsp Lemon Juice
- Salt and Pepper, to taste

Method:

1. Preheat your grill to 350 degrees F.
2. Peel the zucchini and slice lengthwise. Season with salt and pepper.
3. Open the grill and coat with cooking spray.
4. Arrange the zucchini on top of the bottom plate and lower the lid.
5. Cook for 2-3 minutes.

6.Meanwhile, combine the remaining ingredients in a large bowl.

7.Transfer the zucchini to cutting bord and chop into pieces.

8.Add to the bowl and toss well to combine.

9.Serve and enjoy!

Nutritional Value:

•Calories 192

•Total Fats 14.6g

•Carbs 12.6g

•Protein 5g

•Fiber: 2.7g

102

PORK AND VEGGIE SALAD

Preparation Time: 2 minutes

Cooking Time: 8 minutes

Servings: 1

Ingredients:

- ½ pound Pork Tenderloin
- 1 Lettuce Head
- 1 Tomato, chopped
- 1 Cucumber, chopped
- 1 can Beans, drained
- 1 Carrot, julienned
- 2 tbsp Olive Oil
- 2 tbsp Sour Cream
- 1 tsp Dijon Mustard
- 1 tsp Lemon Juice
- 1 tbsp Honey
- Salt and Pepper, to taste

Method:

1. Preheat your grill to medium-high.
2. Cut the pork into strips and season with salt and pepper.

3. Coat the grill with cooking spray and arrange the pork onto the bottom plate.

4. Lower the lid so you can cut the cooking time in half and cook for 5 minutes.

5. When done, transfer to a cutting board.

6. If you want to, you can cut the pork into even smaller bite-sized pieces at this point.

7. Add the oil, lemon juice, mustard, honey, sour cream, and some salt and pepper, to a large bowl.

8. Mix well to combine and add the veggies.

9. Toss well to coat.

10. Top the salad with the grilled pork.

11. Enjoy!

Nutritional Value:
- Calories 240
- Total Fats 18g
- Carbs 15g
- Protein 20g
- Fiber: 2g

103

RIB EYE STEAK SALAD

Preparation Time: 10 minutes
   Cooking Time: 5 minutes
   Servings: 4
   Ingredients:
   •1 ½ pounds Rib Eye Steaks
   •¼ cup Fish Sauce
   •½ cup Mint Leaves
   •4 tbsp Lime Juice
   •½ cup Coriander Leaves
   •1 Lettuce Head
   •1 cup halved Cherry Tomatoes
   •Salt and Pepper, to taste
   Method:
   1.Preheat your grill to 375 degrees F. Spray with cooking spray.
   2.Season the steak with salt and pepper and cut into strips.
   3.When ready, arrange the steak onto the bottom plate.
   4.Lower the lid and cook for 4-5 minutes, depending on the doneness you wish to achieve. Transfer to a plate.
   5.Chop the lettuce and add to a bowl.

6.Add the rest of the ingredients and toss well to combine and coat.

7.Top the salad with the grilled steak.

8.Serve and enjoy!

Nutritional Value:

•Calories 350

•Total Fats 30g

•Carbs 10g

•Protein 31g

•Fiber: 1g

104

CHICKEN CAESAR SALAD

Preparation Time: 10 minutes
Cooking Time: 6 minutes
Servings: 4
Ingredients:
•4 Chicken Breasts, boneless and skinless
•1 Lettuce Head
•1/3 cup Olive Oil
•½ tsp Dijon Mustard
•1 tsp Lemon Juice
•½ cup grated Parmesan Cheese
•½ tsp Anchovy Paste
•1 tsp Red Wine Vinegar
•1 tsp Worcestershire Sauce
•1 cup Croutons
•1 tsp Honey
•Salt and Pepper, to taste
Method:
1.Preheat your grill to medium-high heat.
2.When the green light turns on, open the grill and coat with cooking spray.

3.Season the chicken with salt and pepper and place onto the bottom plate.

4.Lower the lid and cook the chicken for 6 full minutes.

5.Transfer to a cutting board and cut into strips.

6.Chop the lettuce head and place in a bowl. Add the chicken and croutons to the bowl.

7.In a smaller bowl, whisk together the remaining ingredients and drizzle the salad with the mixture.

8.Serve and enjoy!

Nutritional Value:

•Calories 540

•Total Fats 35g

•Carbs 15g

•Protein 45g

•Fiber: 4g

105

GREEK GRILLED SALMON SALAD

Preparation Time: 10 minutes

Cooking Time: 8 minutes

Servings: 4

Ingredients:

- 1-pound Salmon Fillets
- 4 cups chopped Lettuce
- 1 Red Onion, sliced
- 1/3 cup Kalamata Olives, pitted
- 1 Cucumber, chopped
- 1 Avocado, sliced
- 2 Tomatoes, chopped
- ½ cup Feta Cheese, crumbled
- 3 tbsp Olive Oil
- 1 tsp Oregano
- 1 tsp Basil
- 2 tbsp Lemon Juice
- Salt and Pepper, to taste

Method:

1. Preheat your grill to medium-high.
2. When ready, open the grill and coat with cooking spray.

3.Season the salmon with salt and pepper and arrange onto the bottom plate.

4.Grill open, for about 4 minutes. Flip over, and grill for another 3 to 4 minutes.

5.Transfer to a cutting board and slice.

6.Place the veggies in a large bowl and toss to combine well.

7.Top the salad with the grilled salmon slices and feta cheese.

8.In a smaller bowl, whisk together the olive oil, lemon juice, oregano, basil, and some salt and pepper. Drizzel over the salad.

9.Serve and enjoy!

Nutritional Value:

•Calories 411

•Total Fats 27g

•Carbs 12g

•Protein 28g

•Fiber: 6g

SANDWICH RECIPES

106

CHICKEN BURGERS

Preparation Time: 10 minutes

Cooking Time: 8 minutes

Servings: 4

Ingredients:

•4 Hamburger Buns

•8 Red Onion Rings

•4 slices of Provolone Cheese

•4 Lettuce Leaves

•1 Avocado, scooped out and mashed

•4 Chicken Breast Halves, boneless and skinless

•1 tbsp Olive Oil

•1 tsp Garlic Powder

•½ tsp Paprika

•¼ tsp Cumin

•¼ tsp Oregano

•¼ tsp Basil

•¼ tsp Turmeric Powder

•Salt and Pepper, to taste

Method:

1.Preheat your grill to medium high.

2.Combine the oil and spices together, and gently rub the meat with this mixture.

3.Open the grill when the green light turns on and place the chicken on top of the bottom grill.

4.Cook for about 4 minutes, then flip over, and cook for another four minutes on the other side.

5.Meanwhile, cut the buns in half and divide the avocado between four halves. Add the lettuce leave on top.

6.Place the chicken on top of the lettuce and top with the cheese and onion rings.

7.Top the sandwich with the remaining bun halves.

8.Serve and enjoy!

Nutritional Value:

•Calories 480

•Total Fats 23g

•Carbs 31g

•Protein 37g

•Fiber: 6g

107

CHICKEN PESTO GRILLED SANDWICH

Preparation Time: 10 minutes

Cooking Time: 4 minutes

Servings: 2

Ingredients:

•4 Slices of Bread

•1 ½ cups shredded Mozzarella Cheese

•½ cup Pesto Sauce

•2 cups cooked and shredded Chicken Meat

•8 Sundried Tomatoes

•1 ½ tbsp Butter

Method:

1.Preheat your grill to medium-high.

2.Combine the pesto and chicken in a bowl.

3.Brush the outsides of the bread with the butter.

4.Divide the pesto/chicken filling between two bread slices.

5.Top with sundried tomatoes and mozzarella cheese.

6.Open the grill and carefully transfer the loaded slices of bread onto the top bottom.

7.Top with the remaining bread slices, carefully.

8.Lower the lid, pressing gently.

9.Let the sandwiches cook for about 3-4 minutes, or until the desired doneness is reached.

10. Serve and enjoy!

Nutritional Value:

- •Calories 725
- •Total Fats 44.5g
- •Carbs 32g
- •Protein 51g
- •Fiber: 7.5g

108

FISH TACOS WITH SLAW AND MANGO SALSA

Preparation Time: 10 minutes

Cooking Time: 6 minutes

Servings: 4

Ingredients:

•4 Tortillas

•1-pound Cod

•3 tbsp butter, melted

•½ tsp Paprika

•¼ tsp Garlic Onion

•1 tsp Thyme

•½ tsp Onion Powder

•½ tsp Cayenne Pepper

•1 tsp Brown Sugar

•1 cup prepared (or store-brought) Slaw

•Salt and Pepper, to taste

Mango Salsa:

•¼ cup diced Red Onions

•Juice of 1 Lime

•1 Mango, diced

•1 Jalapeno Pepper, deseeded and minced

•1 tbsp chopped Parlsey or Cilantro

Method:

1.Preheat your grill to medium.

2.Brush the butter over the cod and sprinkle with the spices.

3.When ready, open the grill, and arrange the cod fillets onto the bottom plate.

4.Lower the lid and cook for about 4-5 minutes in total.

5.Transfer to a plate and cut into chunks.

6.Place all of the mango salsa ingredients in a bowl and mix to combine.

7.Assemble the tacos by adding slaw, topping with grilled cod, and adding a tablespoon or so of the mango salsa.

8.Enjoy!

Nutritional Value:

•Calories 323

•Total Fats 12g

•Carbs 31g

•Protein 24g

•Fiber: 3g

109

SIMPLE PORK CHOP SANDWICH

Preparation Time: 10 minutes

Cooking Time: 7 minutes

Servings: 4

Ingredients:

•4 Hamburger Buns

•4 Cheddar Slices

•4 boneless Pork Chop

•Salt and Pepper, to taste

•4 tbsp Mayonnaise

Method:

1.Preheat your grill to 375 degrees F.

2.When the green light turns on, open the grill.

3.Season the pork chops with salt and pepper and arrange onto the bottom plate.

4.Lower the lid, and cook the meat closed, for about 5-6 minutes.

5.Open the lid and place a slice of cheddar on top of each chop.

6.Cook for another minute or so, uncovered, until the cheese starts to melt.

7.Spread a tbsp of mayonnaise onto the insides of each bun.

8.Place the cheesy pork chop inside and serve.

9.Enjoy!

Nutritional Value:

•Calories 510

•Total Fats 30.6g

•Carbs 18.4g

•Protein 42g

•Fiber: 5g

110

THE GREATEST BUTTER BURGER RECIPE

Preparation Time: 10 minutes
Cooking Time: 11 minutes
Servings: 6
Ingredients:
•2 pounds Ground Chuck Meat
•1 ½ tsp minced Garlic
•6 tbsp Butter
•2 tbsp Worcestershire Sauce
•1 tsp Salt
•½ tsp Pepper
•6 Hamburger Buns
•Veggie Toppings of Choice
Method:
1.Preheat your grill to medium-high.
2.Meanwhile, place the meat, garlic, sauce, salt, and pepper, in a bowl.
3.Mix with your hands to incorporate well. Make six patties out of the mixture.
4.Into each patty, press about one tablespoon into the center.
5.Open the grill and coat with some cooking spray.

6.Arrange the patties onto the bottom plate and cook for 6 minutes.

7.Flip over and cook for 5 more minutes.

8.Serve in hamburger buns with desired veggie toppings.

9.Enjoy!

Nutritional Value:

•Calories 595

•Total Fats 48g

•Carbs 25g

•Protein 27g

•Fiber: 1.5g

111

CHEESY BUFFALO AVOCADO SANDWICH

Preparation Time: 15 minutes

Cooking Time: 4 minutes

Servings: 4

Ingredients:

- 1 Avocado
- 2 Bread Slices
- 2 slices Cheddar Cheese
- 1 tbsp Butter

Buffalo Sauce:

- 4 tbsp Hot Sauce
- 1 tbs White Vinegar
- ¼ cup Butter
- ¼ tsp Salt
- 1 tsp Cayenne Pepper
- ¼ tsp Garlic Salt

Method:

1. Preheat your grill to 375 degrees F.

2. Meanwhile, peel the avocado, scoop out the flash, and mash it with a fork.

3.Spread the avocado onto a bread slice, and top with the cheddar cheese.

4.Spread the butter onto the outside of the other bread slice.

5.Top the sandwich with the buttery slice, with the butter-side up.

6.Grease the bottom cooking plate and place the sandwich there, with the butter-side up.

7.Lower the lid, press, and let the sandwich grill for about 4 minutes.

8.Meanwhile, whisk together all of the sauce ingredients.

9.Serve the sandwich with the Buffalo sauce and enjoy!

Nutritional Value:
•Calories 485
•Total Fats 24g
•Carbs 35g
•Protein 8g
•Fiber: 3g

112

BUTTERY PEPPERONI GRILLED CHEESE SANDWICH

Preparation Time: 10 minutes

Cooking Time: 5 minutes

Servings: 2

Ingredients:

•4 slices of Bread

•4 slices of Mozzarella Cheese

•4 tbsp Butter

•18 Pepperoni Slices

Method:

1.Preheat your grill to medium-high.

2.Meanwhile, brush each slice of bread with a tablespoon of butter. It seems like too much, but the taste is just incredible.

3.Divide the mozzarella and pepperoni among the insides of two bread slices.

4.Top the sandwich with the other slices of bread, keeping the buttery side up.

5.When the green light appears, open the grill.

6.Place the sandwiches carefully onto the bottom plate.

7.Lower the lid, and gently press.

8.Allow the sandwich to cook for 4-5 minutes.

9.Open the lid, transfer to a serving plate, cut in half, and serve. Enjoy!

Nutritional Value:
- Calories 625
- Total Fats 46g
- Carbs 29g
- Protein 22g
- Fiber: 2g

SIDE DISHES RECIPES

113

ITALIAN-SEASONED GRILLED VEGGIES

Preparation Time: 15 minutes

Cooking Time: 8 minutes

Servings: 8

Ingredients:

- •1 Zucchini, cut into chunks
- •1 Squash, cut into chunks
- •8 ounces Button Mushrooms, quartered
- •1 Red Bell Pepper, chopped
- •1 Red Onion, cut into chunks
- •2 tbsp Balsamic Vinegar
- •4 tbsp Olive Oil
- •2 tbsp Italian Seasoning
- •4 tbsp grated Parmesan Cheese
- •Juice of 1 Lemon
- •½ tsp Garlic Powder

Method:

1.Preheat your grill to medium-high heat.

2.In a bowl, place all of the ingredient, except the Parmesan Cheese.

3.With your hands, mix well so that each chunk of veggie is coated with oil and seasoning.

4.Thread the veggie chunks onto metal skewers (You can also use soaked wooden ones).

5.When the grill is ready, open the lid, and arrange the skewers onto the bottom plate.

6.Without covering the lid, cook for about 4 minutes.

7.Flip the skewers over and cook for another 3-4 minutes.

8.Serve sprinkled with Parmesan cheese and enjoy!

Nutritional Value:

•Calories 110

•Total Fats 8g

•Carbs 7.5g

•Protein 3g

•Fiber: 2.5g

114

BRUSSEL SPROUT SKEWERS

Preparation Time: 10 minutes

Cooking Time: 7 minutes

Servings: 8

Ingredients:

•24 Brussel Sprouts

•2 tbsp Balsamic Glaze

•4 tbsp Olive Oil

•½ tsp Garlic Powder

•Salt and Pepper, to taste

Method:

1.Preheat your grill to 375 degrees F.

2.In the meantime, trim the brussel sprouts and cut the in half.

3.Thread onto soaked wooden or metal skewers.

4.Drizzle with olive oil and sprinkle with the seasonings.

5.Place onto the bottom plate and cook uncovered for 4 minutes.

6.Turn over and cook for another 3 minutes or so.

7.Serve as desired and enjoy!

Nutritional Value:

- Calories 92
- Total Fats 6g
- Carbs 6g
- Protein 1g
- Fiber: 2g

115

GARLICKY MUSHROOM SKEWERS WITH BALSAMIC VINEGAR

Preparation Time: 40 minutes

Cooking Time: 4 minutes

Servings: 4

Ingredients:

•2 pounds Button Mushrooms, halved

•1 tbsp Tamari Sauce

•2 tbsp Balsamic Vinegar

•½ tsp Dried Thyme

•2 large Garlic Cloves, minced

•Salt and Pepper, to taste

Method:

1.Place the tamari, balsamic, thyme, and garlic, in a bowl.

2.Season with some salt and pepper and mix well to combine.

3.Add the mushrooms and toss to coat them well.

4.Cover the bowl and place in the fridge for about 30 minutes.

5.While the mushrooms are marinating, soak your wooden skewers in water to prevent burning.

6.Preheat your grill to 375 degrees F.

7.Thread the mushrooms onto your skewers and place on top of the bottom plate.

8.Grill for 2 minutes, then flip over, and grill for another two minutes, or until tender.

9.Serve and enjoy!

Nutritional Value:

•Calories 62

•Total Fats 1g

•Carbs 9g

•Protein 7g

•Fiber: 2g

116

GRILLED ZUCCHINI

Preparation Time: 65 minutes

Cooking Time: 6 minutes

Servings: 4

Ingredients:

- 1-pound Zucchini
- 1 tbsp Lemon Juice
- 2 Garlic Cloves, minced
- 2 tbsp Olive Oil
- 1 tsp Italian Seasoning
- Salt and Pepper, to taste

Method:

1. Trim and peel the zucchini. Cut into thick slices and place in a bowl.

2. Add all of the remaining ingredients and mix well so that the zucchini slices are completely coated.

3. Cover the bowl and place in the fridge for about one hour.

4. Menawhile, preheat your HB grill to 375 degrees F.

5. When the green light turns on, open the grill and place the zucchini slices onto the bottom plate.

6.Cook with the lid off, for three minutes. Flip over and cook for another three minutes.

7.Serve as desired and enjoy!

Nutritional Value:

•Calories 76

•Total Fats 7g

•Carbs 1g

•Protein 0g

•Fiber: 0g

117

BALSAMIC-GLAZED CARROTS

Preparation Time: 10 minutes

Cooking Time: 6 minutes

Servings: 10

Ingredients:

•2 pounds Carrots, boiled for 3-4 minutes

•3 tbsp Balsamic Vinegar

•1 tsp ground Ginger

•1 tsp Thyme

•1 ½ tbsp Maple Syrup

•½ tbsp Lime Juice

•Salt and Pepper, to taste

Method:

1.Preheat your grill to 400 degrees F.

2.Meanwhile, cut the carrots in half lengthwise.

3.Place the remaining ingredients in a bowl and whisk well to combine.

4.Brush the carrots with the mixture, on all sides.

5.When the green light is on, open the grill and spray with some cooking spray.

6.Arrange the carrots on top of the bottom plate and cook for 3 minutes.

7.Flip over and cook for 3 more minutes on the other side.

8.Serve and enjoy!

Nutritional Value:

•Calories 50

•Total Fats 1g

•Carbs 12g

•Protein 1g

•Fiber: 3g

118

MAYO & PARMESAN CORN ON THE COB

Preparation Time: 5 minutes

Cooking Time: 15 minutes

Servings: 4

Ingredients:

•4 Ears of Corn

•1 cup grated Parmesan Cheese

•½ cup Mayonnaise

•Juice of 1 Lemon

•1 cup Sour Cream

•½ tsp Cayenne Pepper

•4 tbsp chopped Cilantro

Method:

1.Preheat your grill to medium-high heat.

2.Clean the corn by removing the husk and silk.

3.When the grill is ready, open the lid and place the corn on top of the bottom plate.

4.Cook for about 10 to 15 minutes, rotating occasionally while grilling.

5.Meanwhile, combine the sour cream, mayonnaise, and cilantro.

6.Brush the grilled corn with this mixture, and generously sprinkle with Parmesan cheese.

7.Drizzle the lime juice over before serving. Enjoy!

Nutritional Value:

•Calories 428

•Total Fats 34g

•Carbs 22g

•Protein 11g

•Fiber: 2g

119

GRILLED AND DRESSED ROMAINE HEAD

Preparation Time: 5 minutes
Cooking Time: 5 minutes
Servings: 4
Ingredients
•2 Hearts of Romaine
•½ cup Olive Oil
•2 Eg Yolks
•2 Whole Garlic Cloves
•½ tsp Dijon Mustard
•2 Anchovies
•3 tbsp Parmesan Cheese
•4 tbsp Lemon Juice
•Salt an Pepper, to taste
Method:
1.Preheat your grill to medium high.
2.Place all of the dressing ingredients to the bowl of your food processor.
3.Pulse until smooth and set aside.
4.When the grill is ready, open the lid and spray with some cooking spray.

5.Place the romaine heart onto the bottom plate and cook for 3 minutes.

6.Flip over and cook for 2 more minutes.

7.Arrange on a large serving plate.

8.Drizzle with the dressing.

9.Enjoy!

Nutritional Value:

•Calories 88

•Total Fats 4g

•Carbs 3g

•Protein 2.5g

•Fiber: 0.4g

SNACK RECIPES

120

VEGGIE SLIDERS

Preparation Time: 10 minutes
Cooking Time: 7 minutes
Servings: 10
Ingredients:
• ½ Red Onion, diced
• ¾ cup cooked Quinoa
• 15 ounces canned Kidney
• ½ cup Walnuts, crushed or ground
• 1 shake Worcestershire Sauce
• 1 tbsp Chili Powder
• Salt and Pepper, to taste
Method:
1. Preheat your grill to 350-375 degrees F.
2. Dump all of the ingredients in a bowl and mix well with your hands to incorporate the mixture.
3. Make about 10 small patties with your hands.
4. When ready, open the grill and coat with cooking spray.
5. Arrange the patties on top of the bottom plate.
6. Lower the lid and cook closed for about 6-7 minutes.
7. Serve on top of a lettuce leaf. Enjoy!

Nutritional Value:
- Calories 89
- Total Fats 4.2g
- Carbs 9g
- Protein 4g
- Fiber: 3g

121

ZUCCHINI ROLLUPS WITH HUMMUS

Preparation Time: 15 minutes

Cooking Time: 3 minutes

Servings: 4

Ingredients:

•2 medium Zucchini

•6 tbsp Hummus

•1 tbsp Olive Oil

•1 Roasted Red Pepper, diced

•Salt and Pepper, to taste

Method:

1.Preheat your grill to medium high.

2.Peel and slice the zucchini lengthwise.

3.Brush with olive oil and season with salt and pepper, generously.

4.Open the grill and arrange the zucchini slices on top.

5.Close the grill and cook for 2-3 minutes.

6.Transfer to a serving plate and let cool a bit until safe to handle.

7.Divide the hummus and red pepper among the grilled zucchini.

8.Roll up and secure the filling with a toothpick.

9.Serve and enjoy!

Nutritional Value:

•Calories 43

•Total Fats 3.1g

•Carbs 3.6g

•Protein 1g

•Fiber: 1g

122

GRILLED TOMATOES WITH GARLIC & PARMESAN

Preparation Time: 10 minutes

Cooking Time: 6 minutes

Servings: 8

Ingredients:

•½ cup grated Parmesan Cheese

•8 small Tomatoes, halved

•1 tsp Garlic Powder

•2 tbsp Olive Oil

•¼ tsp Onion Powder

•Salt and Pepper, to taste

Method:

1.Preheat your grill to 350 degrees F.

2.Combine the oil, garlic powder, onion powder, and salt and pepper, in a bowl.

3.Brush the tomatoes with this mixture.

4.Open the grill and arrange the tomatoes onto the plate.

5.Cook for 3 minutes, then flip over and cook for 2 more minutes.

6.Top with the parmesan cheese and cook for an additional minute.

7.Serve and enjoy!

Nutritional Value:

•Calories 78
•Total Fats 5.6g
•Carbs 4.5g
•Protein 3.4g
•Fiber: 1g

123

GRILLED MELON WITH HONEY & LIME

Preparation Time: 10 minutes

Cooking Time: 6 minutes

Servings: 4

Ingredients:

•½ small Melon

•2 tbsp Honey

•Juice of 1 Lime

•Pinch of Salt

•Pinch of Pepper

Method:

1.Preheat your grill to medium high.

2.In the meantime, peel the melon and cut into wedges.

3.When the green light appears, open the grill and coat with cooking spray.

4.Arrange the melon wedges onto the bottom plate of your HB grill.

5.Cook for about 3 minutes.

6.Flip over and cook for another three minutes.

7.Whisk together the honey, lime, salt, and pepper, and brush the grilled melon with this mixture.

8.Serve and enjoy!

Nutritional Value:

•Calories 92

•Total Fats 2g

•Carbs 24g

•Protein 2g

•Fiber: 4g

124

BACON-WRAPPED PEPPERS

Preparation Time: 10 minutes

Cooking Time: 6 minutes

Servings: 4

Ingredients:

•4 ounces Cream Cheese, softened

•8 smallish Peppers

•4 Bacon Slices

Method:

1.Preheat your grill to 375 degrees F.

2.Cut of the top of the peppers and fiscard the seeds.

3.Fill the peppers with the cheese.

4.Cut the bacon slices in half, lengthwise, and wrap each pepper with it.

5.Open the grill and unlock the hinge.

6.Make sure the kickstand is in place.

7.Arrange the peppers onto the grill and cook for about 3 minutes.

8.Flip over and cook for another three minutes.

9.Serve and enjoy!

Nutritional Value:

- Calories 156
- Total Fats 13g
- Carbs 5g
- Protein 1.1g
- Fiber: 6.2g

125

GRILLED PINEAPPLE WITH COCONUT SAUCE

Preparation Time: 10 minutes

Cooking Time: 8 minutes

Servings: 4

Ingredients:

- 1 large Pineapple
- 1 ½ tsp Cornstarch
- 2 tbsp Coconut Rum
- 1 tbsp Butter
- 1 tbsp Cream of Coconut

Method:

1. Preheat your grill to medium high.

2. In the meantime, prepare the pineapple. Peel and slice into the size of your preference.

3. Thread the pineapple slices onto soaked skewers and open the grill.

4. Arrange on top of the bottom plate and grill for about 4 minutes per side.

5. In the meantime, whisk together the remaining ingredients in a saucepan.

6. Place over medium heat and cook until slightly thickened.

7.Serve the pineapple alongside the sauce.

8.Enjoy!

Nutritional Value:

•Calories 235

•Total Fats 10g

•Carbs 34g

•Protein 2g

•Fiber: 3g

126

SHRIMP & PINEAPPLE KABOBS

Preparation Time: 25 minutes

Cooking Time: 6 minutes

Servings: 6

Ingredients:

•18 large Shrimp, cleaned

•4 tbsp Honey

•4 tbsp Soy Sauce

•12 Pineapple Chunks

•4 tbsp Balsamic Vinegar

•Salt and Pepper, to taste

Method:

1.Thread the shrimp and pineapple onto skewers (no need to soak them) and place in a Ziploc bag.

2.In a bowl, whisk together the remaining ingredients.

3.Pour the mixture over the shrimp and pinapple.

4.Seal the bag and let marinate in the fridge for 15 minutes.

5.Meanwhile, preheat your grill to medium.

6.Once ready, open the grill and arrange the skewers onto the bottom plate.

7.Grill without lowering the lid, for 3 minutes per side.

8.Serve and enjoy!

Nutritional Value:

•Calories 61
•Total Fats 1g
•Carbs 11g
•Protein 4g
•Fiber: 1g

DESSERT RECIPES

127

GRILLED PEACHES WITH VANILLA ICE CREAM

Preparation Time: 10 minutes
Cooking Time: 6 minutes
Servings: 4

Ingredients:
•4 Large Peaches
•4 Scoops of Vanilla Ice Cream
•2 tsp Honey
•1 tbsp Butter, melted

Method:
1.Preheat your grill to medium high.
2.Cut the peaches in half and discard the pit.
3.Brush with butter on all sides, and place on top of the bottom grilling grate.
4.Cook for 3 minutes, then flip over, and cook for additional 3 minutes.
5.Transfer to a serving plate.
6.Wait a minute (so that your ice cream doesn't melt immediately), then drizzle with honey and add a scoop of ice cream on top.
7.Enjoy!

Nutritional Value:
- Calories 201
- Total Fats 4g
- Carbs 23g
- Protein 3g
- Fiber: 1g

128

GRILLED WATERMELON & CREAM

Preparation Time: 10 minutes

Cooking Time: 4 minutes

Servings: 8

Ingredients:

•1 medium Watermelon

•3 cups Whipped Cream

•2 tbsp chopped Mint

Method:

1.Preheat your grill to medium high.

2.Peel the melon and cut into wedges. Discard seeds if there are any.

3.Open the grill and arrange the wedges on top of the bottom plate.

4.Lower te lid and cook for 3-4 minutes.

5.Open and transfer to a cutting board.

6.Cut into smaller chunks and let cool.

7.Divide among 8 serving glasses.

8.Top with whipped cream and mint leaves.

9.Enjoy!

Nutritional Value:

- Calories 323
- Total Fats 17.3g
- Carbs 44g
- Protein 4.4g
- Fiber: 2.2g

129

CINNAMON SUGAR GRILLED APRICOTS

Preparation Time: 10 minutes

Cooking Time: 6 minutes

Servings: 4

Ingredients:

•6 smallish Apricots

•1 tbsp Butter, melted

•3 tbsp Brown Sugar

•½ tbsp Cinnamon

Method:

1.Preheat your grill to 350 degrees F.

2.Cut the apricots in half and discard the seeds.

3.When ready, open the grill and coat with cooking spray.

4.Arrange the apricots and cook for 3 minutes.

5.Flip over and cook for 3 minutes more.

6.Meanwhile, whisk together the butter, sugar, and cinnamon.

7.Transfer the grilled apricots to a serving plate.

8.Drizzle the sauce over.

9.Enjoy!

Nutritional Value:

- Calories 92
- Total Fats 2g
- Carbs 17g
- Protein 1g
- Fiber: 1g

130

CHOCOLATE-COVERED GRILLED STRAWBERRIES

Preparation Time: 10 minutes

Cooking Time: 6 minutes

Servings: 4

Ingredients:

•12 Large Strawberries

•3 ounces Chocolate

•1 tbsp Butter

Method:

1.Preheat your grill to 350 degrees F.

2.Clean and hull the strawberries.

3.When the green light appears, arrange the strawberries onto the plate.

4.Grill for about 6 minutes, rotating occasionally for even cooking.

5.Melt the chocolate and butter in a microwave. Stir to combine.

6.Coat the grilled strawberries with the melted chocolate and arrange on a platter.

7.Let harden before consuming.

8.Enjoy!

Nutritional Value:

- •Calories 146
- •Total Fats 8g
- •Carbs 18.3g
- •Protein 1.4g
- •Fiber: 1.6g

131

APPLE CRIPS IN FOIL

Preparation Time: 15 minutes

Cooking Time: 20 minutes

Servings: 8

Ingredients:

•4 Apples, sliced

•½ cup Flour

•4 tbsp Sugar

•2 tsp Cinnamon

•½ cup Quick Oats

•½ cup Butter, melted

•½ cup Brown Sugar

•½ tsp Baking Powder

Method:

1.Preheat your grill to 350 degrees F.

2.Prepare 4 aluminium foil squares (about 8x12 inches each).

3.Divide the apple slices among the foil and sprinkle with sugar and cinnamon.

4.In a bowl, combine the remaining ingredients well.

5.Divide the mixture evenly among the foil packets.

6.Carefully foil the packets, sealing so the filling stays inside.

7.When ready, open the grill and unlock the hinge.

8.Lay the griddle grate on top of your counter and place the foils there.

9.Cook for about 10 minutes.

10. Then, flip over, and cook for 10 minutes more.

11. Carefully open the packets and let sit for about 10 minutes before consuming.

12. Enjoy!

Nutritional Value:

•Calories 318

•Total Fats 7g

•Carbs 51g

•Protein 2g

•Fiber: 3g

132

FRUITY SKEWERS

Preparation Time: 10 minutes
Cooking Time: 6 minutes
Servings: 4

Ingredients:

- •1 Pineapple, cut into chunks
- •12 Strawberries, halved
- •2 Mangos, cut into chunks
- •½ cup Orange Juice
- •2 tbsp Honey
- •1 tbsp Brown Sugar
- •1 tbsp Butter

Method:

1.Preheat your grill to medium high.

2.Thread the fruit chunks onto soaked skewers.

3.Open the grill and place the skewers on the bottom grilling plate.

4.Cook for 3 minutes.

5.Flip over and cook for additional 3 minutes.

6.Meanwhile, combine the remaining ingredients in a small saucepan, and cook until slightly thickened.

7.Drizzle over the fruit skewers and serve. Enjoy!

Nutritional Value:

•Calories 180
•Total Fats 4g
•Carbs 22g
•Protein 2g
•Fiber: 1g

133

COCONUT-COATED PINEAPPLE

Preparation Time: 10 minutes

Cooking Time: 6 minutes

Servings: 6

Ingredients:

•1 Pineapple

•2 tbsp Honey

•1 tbsp Coconut Cream

•1/3 cup Shredded Coconut

Method:

1.Preheat your grill to medium high.

2.Meanwhile, peel and slice the coconut.

3.Thread each slice onto a soaked skewer.

4.Open the grill and arrange the skewers on top of the bottom plate.

5.Cook for 3 minutes per side.

6.Meanwhile, whisk together the honey and coconut cream.

7.Brush the pineapple with the mixture.

8.Place the coconut in a shallow bowl.

9.Coat the brushed pineapple with the coconut, on all sides.

10. Serve and enjoy!

Nutritional Value:
- Calories 75
- Total Fats 20g
- Carbs 20g
- Protein 0g
- Fiber: 1g

EXTRA RECIPES

134

GRILLED CORN SALAD

Ingredients:
- 1 clove garlic
- 4 ears of corn, shucked, grilled
- 1 jalapeno, seeds removed, finely diced
- 1/2 red onion, chopped
- 1/2 cup English cucumber, chopped
- 1 lime, juiced
- 1/2 cup sour cream
- 2 tablespoons white wine vinegar
- 1/2 bunch cilantro, chopped
- 1 avocado, diced
- 1/4 cup greek yogurt or mayonnaise
- 1/4 teaspoon kosher salt
- 1/4 teaspoon freshly ground black pepper
- 1 cup cherry tomatoes, halved

Instructions:
- Preheat the grill to medium heat.
- Put the corn, still with its husks, on the grill, cover and cook for 20 minutes rotating the ears of corn every 5 minutes or so.
- Meanwhile, in a large bowl, toss to combine the garlic,

jalapeno, and a large pinch of kosher salt. Add the lime zest, lime juice, sour cream, and mayonnaise or Greek yogurt and toss to combine. Add the avocado, tomatoes, chives, and cilantro and mix gently to combine.

•Remove corn from grill. When cool enough to handle, remove the silk and cut the kernels from the ears directly into the bowl with a knife. Toss to combine. Spice with salt and pepper.

135

GRILLED TEQUILA LIME SHRIMP TACOS

Ingredients:
Marinade :
- •1 pound peeled and deveined shrimp SAUCE
- •1/4 cup lime juice
- •1/2 cup tequila
- •2 tablespoons lime juice
- •1/2 teaspoon salt
- •1 teaspoon dried crushed red pepper
- •1/2 ground cumin
- •1/2 teaspoon ground cumin
- •1/4 teaspoon black pepper
- •3 garlic cloves, minced
- •1/2 cup mayonnaise
- •1/2 teaspoon salt
- • 1 teaspoon chili powder
Tacos :
- •1 medium sweet onion, quartered
- •6 to 8 small corn tortillas
- •1 green pepper, seeded, halved
- •1 yellow pepper, seeded, halved

- 1/4 cup chopped cilantro
- 8 wooden skewers
- 1 avocado, cut into strips
- 1 red pepper, seeded, halved
- 1 tablespoon oil

Instructions:

- In a 1-gallon resealable plastic bag, add tequila, lemon juice, garlic, crushed red pepper, cumin, salt, pepper, and shrimp. Shake the bag and refrigerate for 1 hour.

- Heat grill to SEARING. Soak the skewers in water for 30 minutes.

- Meanwhile, in a small bowl, stir the mayonnaise, lemon juice, chili powder, cumin, and salt until well combined. Cover and refrigerate until ready to assemble.

- Roast the peppers and onions for 15 minutes, turning once until tender. Remove from the grill and place the onion in a bowl. Cut the peppers; add to the onions and cover until ready to serve.

- Drain the shrimp and discard the marinade. Thread 6 shrimp on each skewer.

- Place 4 skewers on the grill and cook for 3 minutes, turning once. Take away from the grill to a plate and cover. Repeat grilling with the remaining skewers.

- Gently coat one side of each tortilla with oil. Broil for 30 seconds to 1 minute to get grill marks and the tortilla will heat up. Repeat with the remaining tortillas.

- Top each tortilla with bell peppers, onions, avocado, shrimp, and cilantro. Drizzle with sauce. Fold in half to serve.

136

GRILLED NEW YORK STRIP STEAKS WITH PEACH CHIMICHURRI

Ingredients:
- 4 New York Strip Steaks
- Pepper to taste
- Coarse salt to taste

For the Peach Chimichurri :
- 2 peaches slightly firm
- 6⅓tbsp extra virgin olive oil divided
- 1 heirloom tomato seeded and chopped
- 4 cloves garlic minced
- ¼ tsp pepper
- 3 tbsp white wine vinegar
- ½ tsp salt
- 1 small bunch of fresh parsley about one cup packed
- ¼ cup Vidalia onion chopped
- ¼ tsp red pepper flakes
- 1 tbsp fresh basil chopped
- 1 tbsp fresh thyme leaves

Instructions:
- Remove the bottom stems from the parsley, rinse and pat dry.

•In the bowl of a food processor, add parsley, garlic, vinegar, fresh thyme, onion, fresh basil, ½ teaspoon salt, ¼ teaspoon pepper, and red pepper flakes.

•Process until smooth, pour into a medium bowl and set aside.

•Heat the grill over medium heat.

•While the grill is heating up, cut the peaches in half, remove the pit and drizzle each side with 1 teaspoon olive oil.

•Roast the peaches for 4 minutes on each side. Let cool.

•Chop the tomatoes, making sure to remove the seeds.

•Next, chop the cooled peaches.

•Stir the remaining 6 tablespoons of olive oil into the chopped herb mixture until just combined. Add the peaches and tomatoes. Cover with plastic wrap and let the mixture sit for 2-3 hours to marinate.

•Preheat the grill to medium heat. Season the steaks with salt and pepper.

•Grill 10-15 minutes on a grill to desired doneness.

•Take away from grill and allow steaks stand for 5 minutes. Pour sauce over steak and serve.

137

GRILLED CAJUN CHICKEN SALAD WITH CREAMY CAJUN DRESSING

Ingredients:

Salad :
- 4-6 cups mixed lettuce greens
- 4 teaspoons Cajun seasoning
- 2 cups grape tomatoes, sliced in half
- 1 English cucumber, diced into thin discs
- 1 avocado, peeled and sliced
- 2 tablespoons olive oil
- 1/2 of a red onion, peeled, diced
- 4 boneless, skinless chicken breasts

Creamy Cajun Dressing :
- Juice from 1/2 a lemon
- 3/4 cup mayonnaise
- 2 teaspoons garlic, minced
- 1 cup buttermilk
- 1-2 teaspoons Cajun seasoning
- 1 tablespoon red wine vinegar
- 1/2 cup sour cream (or Greek yogurt)
- 1 teaspoon Kosher salt
- Freshly ground black pepper, to taste

•1/4 cup freshly grated Parmesan

Instructions:

•Prepare the salad constituents by washing and drying the veggies, then chop the cucumbers into thin discs, chopping the grape tomatoes in half, and cutting the onion into thin strips.

•Make Creamy Cajun Salad Dressing by processing all the dressing ingredients together in a blender or food processor until completely combined. I would recommend starting with 1 teaspoon of Cajun seasoning and increasing the amount until you reach your desired level of spiciness. Refrigerate for 20 minutes before serving.

•Heat grill over medium-high heat. Place the chicken breasts on a baking sheet or large plate and pat dry. Drizzle lightly with olive oil and rub the chicken to coat it evenly. Sprinkle 1/2 teaspoon Cajun seasoning over the top of each chicken breast, flip the chicken, and sprinkle each chicken breast with another 1/2 teaspoon Cajun seasoning so the chicken is evenly coated on both sides.

•Place the chicken breasts straight on the hot side of the grill and grill for 5 minutes per side, until the internal temperature of the breasts reaches 160F. You can also check if the chicken is done by making a small cut in the thickest part to see if it is opaque in the center, or by pressing the thick end of the chicken with your finger to see if there is any resistance. If chicken is done, take away from the grill and allow to stand for 5 minutes.

•Prepare each salad plate by dividing the lettuce among four large plates. Place the tomatoes, onions, cucumbers and avocado on top of the lettuce, then cut each chicken breast into strips and place on top of each salad. Serve with Creamy Cajun Dressing.

138

GRILLED SHRIMP & AVOCADO SALAD

Ingredients:
- 1/2 medium white onion minced
- Salt and pepper to taste
- 1/2 pound shrimp seasoned in Vulcan's Fire Salt peeled, grilled, chopped
- 1 pint cherry tomatoes quartered
- 2 cucumbers quartered, chopped
- 2 avocados chopped
- 1/2 cup fresh lemon juice

Instructions:
- Peel and devein shrimp, then pass two wooden skewers through each shrimp. Place 3-4 shrimp per double skewer.
- Then season with Vulcan's Fire Salt and grill on browning mode for 3-4 minutes on each side until fully cooked and no longer pink.
- While the shrimp is cooking, mix in all the other ingredients except the avocado.
- When the shrimp are done, cut them into small pieces and let them cool.

•Once the shrimp cool, add that and the avocado to the cucumber mixture. Give it a quick stir and serve!

GRILLED PEACHES WITH ICE CREAM

Ingredients:
- 2 large ripe peaches, sliced in half
- 4 scoops vanilla ice cream
- 1 tablespoon oil
- Honey, to drizzle over the grilled peaches

Instructions:
- Heat a grill over medium-high heat. Brush the cut halves of each peach with oil, then place cut side down on the grill and close the lid.
- Cook 3-4 minutes until grill marks appear, then flip peaches over and cook for another 3-4 minutes until peaches are heated through and peaches are soft.
- Take away the peaches from the grill and sprinkle with a pint-sized honey, then coat individual peach half with a scoop of ice cream.
- Serve and enjoy.

COBB SIRLOIN KEBABS WITH RANCH VINAIGRETTE

Ingredients:
- 1 clove garlic minced
- 4 oz sharp cheddar cheese block, chopped, 2-inch portions
- ¼ cup extra virgin olive oil
- Sea salt and pepper to taste
- 1 pint golden cherry tomatoes keep whole
- 1 ½ lbs top sirloin diced, 2-inch chunks
- 3 large eggs
- Bamboo skewers
- ⅓ cup light ranch dressing
- Medium lemon juiced and zested
- 1 tablespoon fresh parsley minced
- 2 red peppers diced into 2-inch chunks
- 3-4 large romaines leaves rinsed and patted dry

Instructions:

•Prepare your medium hard-boiled eggs (firm white and semi-firm yolk). Place the eggs in a tiny container and layer with cold water.

•Bring the water to a full boil, then turn off the heat, cover with a lid, and set the timer for 6 minutes. When the timer rings, immediately place the eggs in an ice bath to stop the cooking process.

•Set aside while you prepare your other ingredients.

•To make the dressing, mix together the ranch dressing, lemon juice, lemon zest, garlic, and half of the fresh parsley. Slowly add the olive oil. Top with the remaining parsley before serving.

•For skewers, soak wooden skewers in water to grill for 10 minutes (or use metal skewers).

•Toss the meat cubes, bell peppers, cherry tomatoes and romaine lettuce in a little olive oil and season lightly with sea salt and fresh ground pepper.

•Place the meat cubes, bell peppers, and cherry tomatoes on a skewer, leaving room for the romaine lettuce and cheese last (but don't add them yet).

•Grill skewers over medium-high heat for 2-3 minutes per side (so steak is medium rare). Place the romaine lettuce leaves on the grill and cook quickly until each side begins to wilt and the ends are browned, about 1 minute per side.

•Remove from the grill, coarsely chop to skewer and reserve. In a grill pan, quickly cook cheese until hot and tender enough to pierce.

•Now add the romaine lettuce and cheese to the kebas. Peel and slice the eggs and place them in a bowl with the kebabs.

•Garnish with fresh parsley and serve with the dressing on the side for dipping.

141

GRILLED CHICKEN AND STEAK FAJITAS

Ingredients:

Fajita Meat & Veggies :

• 2-3 red and yellow bell peppers, stem and membranes removed and chopped into quarters

• 1 large onion, sliced into 1/2-inch slices

• 1 lb. chicken and steak

Marinade :

• 1/4 teaspoon ground black pepper

• 3 teaspoons vinegar

• 2 cloves garlic, finely minced

• 3/4 teaspoon salt

• 1/2 teaspoon cayenne pepper

• 1/4 teaspoon onion powder

• 1/2 teaspoon chipotle chili powder

• 2 tablespoons vegetable oil

• 1-2 teaspoons liquid smoke

• 1/3 cup water

• 1/4 cup fresh lime juice

• 2 teaspoons soy sauce

Instructions:

•Place meat and vegetables in separate large ziploc bags. In a bowl, combine all the marinade ingredients and beat well. Reserve 3-4 tablespoons of marinade for later, then use the remaining marinade, add a splash to the veggies for a light coating, then add the remaining marinade to the meat. Marinate in the refrigerator for 4-6 hours.

•Preheat the grill over medium-high heat. When the grill is hot, place everything at the same time. Cook meat for a few minutes on each side until cooked through (165 degrees F for chicken and 135 degrees F for medium-rare steak and 140 degrees F for medium). Cook vegetables until tender, crisp, and slightly charred.

• Remove the meat and vegetables from the grill and cut them into strips on a cutting board. Drizzle with reserved marinade before serving with any of the following: flour tortillas, guacamole, sour cream, diced tomatoes, shredded cheese, black beans, cilantro-lime or Spanish rice, and pico de gallo.

142

ITALIAN PEPPERONI LOVERS PIZZA

We are bringing this one to you all the way from Greece. This wonderful delight is something you would make on a nice movie night. Crispy crust, simple and quick and great to eat.

Prep Time: 5 Minutes

Cook Time: 10 Minutes

Servings: 6

Ingredients:

- 2 tbsp. cooking spray (or olive oil)
- 1 poun d fresh pizza dough
- 1/3 cu p basil pesto
- 1 tbsp. garlic powder
- 12 oz. fresh mozzarella (shredded)
- 25 slices of pepperoni
- Italian dressing (to dip)

Directions:

- Divide the pizza dough into 6 sections.
- Plug in the panini press and make sure it's set to lay flat.
- Tear a sheet of aluminum foil, the same size of your panini press.
- Brush or spray the oil on the foil sheet.

- Stretch 1 piece of dough into a round shape. May have to repeat for the dough has elastic features.
- Spread two to three tablespoons of pesto on the stretched dough.
- Layer the pepperoni, add cheese then add more pepperoni on t op.
- Put the foil on the panini press. Close the lid, allowing the upper plate to hover about 1 inch above the pizza. (if you don't have a panini press that has adjustable height, you might try balling up some foil 1-inch spacers by).
- Grill the pizza until the dough is cooked, cheese is melted/bubbly and lightly brown. About 6 to 8 minutes. Italian dressing to dip!

143

GRILLED STRAWBERRY PANZANELLA

Ingredients:
- •1 loaf, day old Ciabatta bread, cut into 1 inch pieces (about 4 cups)
- •1 lb fresh Strawberries, 8 - 10 sliced and the rest to use in dressing
- •Salt, to taste
- •1/2 cup fresh Basil
- •Pepper, to taste
- •1/2 Red Onion, sliced

For the Dressing :
- •1 tbsp Balsamic Vinegar
- •4 - 6 Strawberries
- •1 - 2 tsp Honey

Instructions:
- •Spray your grill with a nonstick spray. Set your grill to brown at 350 ° F.
- •Add the diced Ciabatta bread and grill for about 2-3 minutes, flip the bread over and continue to grill for an additional 3-5 minutes or until toasted and starting to take on some color.

•Lightly spray grill again, add sliced strawberries, and cook 2-3 minutes on each side.

•Combine roasted strawberries and ciabatta in large serving bowl.

•Add the sliced red onions and season with salt and pepper.

•Prepare the Dressing by mashing the Strawberries together with the Balsamic Vinegar with a fork. If the strawberries are not very sweet, add the honey and mix well.

•Mix the Strawberry Balsamic Dressing together with the Panzanella and add the fresh Basil.

•Serve and enjoy!

144

GARLIC LIME GRILLED SEA BASS

Ingredients:
- Four fresh or thawed 4 oz skin-on sea bass fillets
- 1 tablespoon of extra virgin olive oil
- 2 garlic cloves, minced
- 4 tablespoons fresh lime juice
- 1 lime, quartered
- Coarse sea salt to taste
- Chopped fresh parsley for garnish
- Olive oil grill spray

Instructions:
- Preheat grill for browning, or an outdoor grill to medium high
- Pour 1 tbsp of lime juice over individual fillet
- Spread garlic evenly on top and sprinkle with sea salt
- Cover and place in the refrigerator for 5 minutes to allow the juice to soak into the fillets. (don't let them sit any longer or they will start to "cook" with the citric acid in the juice and you will have ceviche instead.
- Grill the fish, skin side down, for 5 minutes,

•Reduce grill heat to 375 degrees.
•Flip and cook 6 to 7 more minutes until fish flakes with fork.
•Garnish with parsley and fresh lime.

145

SUCCULENT BASIL PESTO PIZZA

Well Pizza is Back! We've got you covered in this department so no need to worry. Quick, easy, fun and deliciously wonderful for you, friends and family! They'll love you for it.

Prep Time: 5 Minutes

Cook Time: 10 Minutes

Servings: 6

Ingredients:

- 2 tbsp. cooking spray (or olive oil)
- 1 poun d fresh pizza dough
- 1/3 cu p basil pesto
- 12 oz. fresh mozzarella (shredded)
- 2 oz. shaved ham

Directions:

- Divide the pizza dough into 6 sections.
- Plug in the panini press and make sure it's set to lay flat.
- Tear a sheet of aluminum foil, the same size of your panini press.
- Brush or spray the oil on the foil sheet.
- Stretch 1 piece of dough into a round shape. May have to repeat for the dough has elastic features.

- Spread two to three tablespoons of pesto on the stretched dough.
- Sprinkle the ham, then top with cheese.
- Put the foil on the panini press. Close the lid, allowing the upper plate to hover about 1 inch above the pizza. (if you don't have a panini press that has adjustable height, you might try balling up some foil 1-inch spacers by).
- Grill the pizza until the dough is cooked, cheese is melted/bubbly and lightly brown. About 6 to 8 minutes. Slice and serve.

146

GRILLED SWEET POTATO WEDGES

Ingredients:
- 1 tbsp Spice Panda Vermont maple seasoning
- 4 sweet potatoes sliced into wedges
- 2 tbsp olive oil

Instructions:
- Preheat the grill over medium-high heat.
- Toss the sweet potato slices in olive oil to coat.
- Rub the wedges with the seasoning mixture
- Grill over medium-high heat for 10 minutes, turning the wedges on all sides until cooked.

147

GRILLED RED PEPPER AND BLACK EYED PEA SALAD

Ingredients:
- 15 oz black eyed peas drained
- 1/2 tablespoon honey
- 4 tablespoons olive oil divided
- 1 teaspoon minced garlic
- Salt and pepper to taste
- 1 tomato chopped
- 6 tablespoons white vinegar
- 2 tbsps chopped fresh cilantro
- 1/4 cup chopped onion
- 1 fresh jalapeno seeded, chopped
- 1 large red bell pepper
- 15 ounces kernel corn drained

Instructions:

•Heat grill over medium high heat. Set to Search.

•Cut the bell pepper in half and remove all the seeds and membranes. Cut in slices. Gently layer the pepper strips with 1 tbsp of oil. Sprinkle with salt and pepper.

•Place the bell pepper strips on the grill skin side down and close the lid. Cook for about 5 to 7 minutes until the skin is tender and slightly charred. Flip them over and cook another 5 minutes until hot and tender.

•Remove and let cool.

•While the peppers are roasting, combine all the other ingredients. Once the peppers are cool, chop them and add them to the black-eyed pea mixture.

•Salt and pepper to taste and serve.

148

HONEY LIME GRILLED CHICKEN

Ingredients:
- 5 pounds chicken legs and thighs

Brine :
- ¼ cup sugar
- ½ cup salt
- 12 cups water

Glaze :
- 1 teaspoon dried crushed red pepper
- ½ teaspoon salt
- 1 ½ cups honey
- 1 tablespoon grated fresh ginger
- 1/4 cup soy sauce
- 1/2 cup lime juice
- Chopped cilantro, for garnish
- 2 tablespoons vegetable oil
- 2 cloves garlic, minced

Instructions:

•Place chicken in gallon-size resealable plastic bags. In a large bowl, combine the water, salt, and sugar. Stir until the salt and sugar dissolve. Pour over bagged chicken. Remove the air from the bags to make sure the chicken is soaked in the brine. Seal bags. Leave the brine in the refrigerator for at least 2 hours or overnight.

•Heat grill to browning or 450 ° F.

•In a medium bowl, combine the glaze ingredients. Reserve half to serve with grilled chicken.

•Grill chicken, skin side down, for about 10 minutes. Flip. Grill 10 minutes and flip again.

•Spread the chicken with glaze. Grill 5 minutes. Turn again so skin side is facing up Brush with glaze and grill until chicken reaches 165 ° F when tested with a meat thermometer.

•Serve chicken with reserved sauce. Sprinkle with cilantro.

149

GRILLED BLACKENED SALMON WITH CREAMY CUCUMBER DILL SAUCE

Ingredients:

Grilled Blackened Salmon :

- 1 tablespoon lemon pepper
- 1 teaspoon seasoned salt
- 3 tablespoons melted butter
- ½ teaspoon ground white pepper
- Lemon wedges
- ¼ teaspoon dry oregano
- 1 ½ tablespoon smoked paprika
- 1 teaspoon cayenne pepper
- ½ teaspoon ground black pepper
- Fresh dill sprigs (optional)
- ¼ teaspoon ancho chili powder
- Olive oil cooking spray
- ¾ teaspoon onion salt
- ½ teaspoon dry basil
- 1 lb salmon fillets

Creamy Cucumber Dill Sauce :

- 1 teaspoon minced garlic
- 2 teaspoons dry dill

•Salt and pepper
•¹/₂ medium cucumber, unseeded, diced
•¹/₄ cup sour cream
•Juice of ¹/₂ lemon
•¹/₄ cup mayonnaise

Instructions:

•Spread the melted butter over the salmon fillets, then lightly season with lemon pepper and seasoned salt.

•Combine the paprika, cayenne pepper, onion salt, basil, white pepper, black pepper, oregano, and chili powder in a small bowl, then rub the seasoning on the skinless side of the salmon. Lightly sprinkle on the sides and bottom where the skin is.

•Refrigerate for about an hour.

•While the salmon is cooling, combine the cucumber, sour cream, mayonnaise, dried dill, minced garlic, lemon juice, salt, and pepper.

• Once mixed, refrigerate to chill and serve.

•Heat the grill to 350 degrees. Brush or drizzle with a light coating of olive oil.

•Once done, place the salmon on the grill skin side down. Close the lid and cook for 5 minutes. Toss the salmon to the other side. Cook for extra 5 minutes.

•Once the internal temperature reaches 145 degrees and the skin is cooked, remove from heat.

•Serve with lemon wedges, creamy cucumber dill sauce, and a sprig of dill.

•Enjoy!

150

PEAR & GORGONZOLA NAAN PIZZA

Ingredients:
- 1 tablespoon balsamic vinegar
- ¼ teaspoon black pepper
- 1 clove garlic, minced
- 2 tablespoons olive oil
- 1 small ripe pear, cored, diced
- 2 medium naan bread
- ¾ teaspoon salt
- 2 cups thinly sliced red onion
- Chopped rosemary for garnish
- 2 teaspoons sugar
- ⅔ cup crumbled Gorgonzola cheese, divided
- 2 tablespoons honey, divided

Instructions:

• In a skillet over medium heat, sizzle the oil. Add the onion and garlic. Cook and stir until onion is clear and garlic is golden brown, about 6 minutes. Add the balsamic vinegar and sugar. Cook 3 to 5 more minutes, stirring occasionally, until mixture thickens.

• Heat grill to 350°F.

•Drizzle 1 tablespoon of honey on each flatbread. Divide onion mixture and pear slices among flatbreads. Sprinkle 1/3 cup Gorgonzola cheese on each flatbread.

•Grill and cook for 12 minutes.

•Take away from grill and drizzle with rosemary (optional). Cut into 8 slices.

GRILLED MARINATED LONDON BROIL

Ingredients:
- 1/2 cup soy sauce
- 1 teaspoon dried oregano
- 2 tablespoons vegetable oil
- 1 tablespoon cider vinegar
- 2 pounds London Broil
- 2 tablespoons ketchup
- 1 clove garlic, minced
- 1 teaspoon ground black pepper

Instructions:

• In a large resealable plastic bag, add the soy sauce, oil, tomato sauce, vinegar, oregano, black pepper, and garlic. Seal the bag and shake.

•Add the meat to the resealable bag. Seal, place in a shallow dish and refrigerate for several hours or overnight.

•Preheat grill to MEDIUM-HIGH heat.

•Grill the steak for 12 to 16 minutes, turning once halfway through or until done. The meat should be cooked medium raw (125 ° F to 130 ° F) to medium (131 ° F to 140 ° F). Let the meat rest for 10 minutes before cutting it finely along the grain.

PARMESAN GRILLED ASPARAGUS

Ingredients:
- Dash garlic powder
- 1 lb fresh asparagus
- 1 tbsp olive oil
- ½ cup grated Parmesan cheese
- 1 tsp fresh lemon zest
- Salt & pepper

Instructions:
- Heat the grill over medium heat and cut a large piece of sturdy aluminum foil
- Rinse the asparagus, pat dry, and snap off the ends.
- Place the asparagus in the center of the foil and drizzle with olive oil.
- Sprinkle the lemon zest and cheese on top and season with garlic powder, salt and pepper.
- Bring the ends together and seal the foil.
- Cook for 10-12 minutes, turning once during cooking.

GRILLED SHRIMP TACOS WITH JALAPEÑO MANGO SLAW

Ingredients:
- 1/4 cup lime juice
- 1/2 tsp salt
- 2 tbsp chopped red onion
- 2 tbsp chopped fresh cilantro
- 1 mango peeled, pitted
- 6 flour tortillas 6-inch
- 2 tbsp McCormick Gourmet Collection Diced Jalapeño Peppers
- 1 pound jumbo shrimp 18 count, skinned and deveined
- 1/4 cup olive oil
- 3 cup shredded cabbage
- 1/2 tsp McCormick Gourmet Collection Garlic Powder
- 1 tbsp honey

Instructions:
- Combine oil, lemon juice, cilantro, jalapeno peppers, honey, garlic powder, and salt in a small bowl with a whisk. Reserve 1/4 of the marinade. Pour the remaining marinade into a large repeatable bag. Add shrimp; flip to coat well. Refrigerate 15 minutes.

•Meanwhile, combine cabbage, mango, and onion in a large bowl. Add reserved marinade; stir to coat. Cover. Refrigerate until ready to serve.

•Brush one side of each tortilla with oil. Grill, oil side down, over medium, heat until lightly browned. Remove the tortillas; cover with a towel to keep warm.

•Remove the shrimp from the marinade. Discard and remaining marinade. Grill shrimp until shrimp turn pink.

•To serve, place 3 shrimp on each tortilla. Top with salad and serve immediately.

154

IT'S THE WEEKEND PIZZA

Sometimes, some of the best things are made simple. This is a pizza you can eat any day of the week, but the flavors of this one will get you going on any weekend occasion.

Prep Time: 5 Minutes

Cook Time: 10 Minutes

Servings: 6

Ingredients:

- 2 tbsp. cooking spray (or olive oil)
- 1 poun d fresh pizza dough
- 1/3 cu p basil pesto
- 1 tbsp. garlic powder
- 12 oz. fresh mozzarella (shredded)
- 12 - 15 slices of pepperoni
- ¼ cup black olives (sliced)
- ¼ cup red onions (sliced)

Directions:

- Divide the pizza dough into 6 sections.
- Plug in the panini press and make sure it's set to lay flat.
- Tear a sheet of aluminum foil, the same size of your panini press.

- Brush or spray the oil on the foil sheet.
- Stretch 1 piece of dough into a round shape. May have to repeat for the dough has elastic features.
- Spread two to three tablespoons of pesto on the stretched dough.
- Layer the pizza evenly with the pepperoni, onion and olive slices. Then shower the cheese on t op.
- Put the foil on the panini press. Close the lid, allowing the upper plate to hover about 1 inch above the pizza. (if you don't have a panini press that has adjustable height, you might try balling up some foil 1-inch spacers by).
- Grill the pizza until the dough is cooked, cheese is melted/bubbly and lightly brown. About 6 to 8 minutes.

155

GRILLED CHICKEN FAJITAS TOSTADAS

Ingredients:
- •2 large onions, sliced
- • 8 corn tostadas
- •2 red bell peppers seeded and sliced into strips
- •5 tbsp extra virgin olive oil
- •2 yellow bell peppers seeded, stripped
- •2 orange bell peppers seeded, stripped
- •2 tbsp fresh lime juice
- •2 lbs fresh organic chicken tenders

Fajitas Seasoning :
- •4 tsp chili powder
- •2 chicken bouillon cubes crushed
- •$\frac{1}{2}$ tsp garlic powder
- •2 tsp paprika
- •2 tbsp cornstarch
- •$\frac{1}{2}$ tsp cumin
- •$\frac{1}{2}$ tsp cayenne pepper
- •2 tsp sea salt
- •1 tsp onion powder
- •2 tsp sugar

Instructions:

•Whisk together all the ingredients for the fajita seasoning and divide in half for the recipe.

•Heat the grill and set to medium-high heat.

• Chop the peppers and onion and reserve in a bowl.

•Add 3 tablespoons of olive oil, 1 tablespoon of lemon juice, and half of the fajita seasoning to the vegetable mixture.

•In a separate bowl, combine the chicken, 2 tablespoons of the olive oil, 1 tablespoon of the lemon juice, and the rest of the fajita seasoning.

•Mix well to coat.

•Grill the mixture separately in a grill pan.

•The chicken takes about 4-5 minutes per side and the pepper mixture a few more minutes.

•Roast until the peppers and onions are tender, stirring a few times while cooking.

•To serve, top corn tostada with bell peppers and onions, chicken, sour cream, salsa, and fresh avocado.

156

EASY GRILLED SALMON IN FOIL PACKETS

Ingredients:
- ½ tsp black pepper
- ½ tsp garlic powder
- 1 lemon sliced into thin slices, unseeded
- 1 tsp coarse salt
- 2 sprigs fresh parsley
- 4 tbsp butter
- 20 oz wild salmon
- ½ oz fresh baby dill

Instructions:
- Pat the salmon dry with a kitchen towel to take away surplus moisture.
- Sprinkle the salmon with salt and reserve.
- Melt the butter and add the garlic powder.
- Preheat the grill to medium heat.
- On a large sheet of sturdy aluminum foil, place a few lemon wedges and a sprig of herbs.
- Top with fish, butter, herbs, and lemon wedges.
- Drizzle with garlic butter.

•Wrap the salmon in foil, bringing the long sides of the foil together and rolling up the edges to seal.

•Grill the salmon for 7-8 minutes, uncover and check if the fish flakes easily with a fork.

•If necessary, grill for a few more minutes uncovered until the fish is done. The fish can take up to 12 minutes depending on the thickness of the fillet. Be careful not to overcook the fish or it may dry out.

GRILLED PEACHES

Ingredients:
- 2 peaches slightly firm, sliced in half
- 2 tsp real maple syrup
- 1 tsp olive oil
- 8 oz plain Greek yogurt full-fat
- 2-3 mint leaves finely chopped

Instructions:
- Cut the peaches in half, remove the pit and brush with olive oil
- Place on a hot grill and cook skin side down for 4 minutes, turn and cook 3-4 more minutes.
- Serve hot with yogurt, maple syrup, and fresh mint.

MOUTHWATERING MARINARA PEPPERONI PIZZA

A traditional dish that you can't get off of your mind. The marinara sauce brings out the flavors of the vegetables nicely in this particular dish. Yes, a classic, but yet delicious. Enjoy!

Prep Time: 5 Minutes

Cook Time: 10 Minutes

Servings: 6

Ingredients:

• 2 tbsp. cooking spray

(or virgin olive oil)

• 1 poun d fresh pizza dough

• 1/3 cu p marinara sauce

• 12 oz. fresh mozzarella (shredded)

• 2 oz. pepperoni

• ½ stick butter (grass fed)

• 1 tbsp. diced green onions

• 1 tsp. garlic powder

Directions:

• Divide the pizza dough into 6 sections.

• Plug in the panini press and make sure it's set to lay flat.

• Tear a sheet of aluminum foil, the same size of your panini press.

• Brush or spray the oil on the foil sheet.

• Stretch 1 piece of dough into a round shape. May have to repeat for the dough has elastic features.

• Spread two to three tablespoons of the marinara sauce on the stretched dough covering evenly.

• Add the pepperoni, garlic, tomatoes, olives then top with cheese.

• Put the foil on the panini press. Close the lid, allowing the upper plate to hover about 1 inch above the pizza. (if you don't have a panini press that has adjustable height, you might try balling up some foil 1-inch spacers by).

• Grill the pizza until the dough is cooked, cheese is melted/bubbly and lightly brown. About 6 to 8 minutes. Set aside to cool.

• Melt butter in a small pan.

• Add garlic and onions. Simmer 2-3 minutes. (for dipping crust)

• Slice and serve.

GRILLED ADOBO CHICKEN

Ingredients:
- •4 pounds chicken leg quarters
- • 3 tbsp minced garlic
- •2 tbsp fresh ground pepper
- •5 bay leaves
- •3/4 cup soy sauce
- •1 1/2 cups water
- •4 tbsp brown sugar
- •3/4 cup vinegar

Instructions:

•Combine the water, vinegar, soy sauce, garlic, brown sugar, pepper, and bay leaves in a very large saucepan. Add the chicken skin side down and bring to a boil over medium-high heat. Cover and simmer for 35 minutes.

•Place the chicken in a bowl and remove the bay leaves. Return mixture to a boil and cook over medium heat about 30 more minutes, stirring occasionally, until thickened.

•Grill the chicken on an oiled barbecue over high heat for 5 minutes per side. Serve with rice and the remaining sauce.

MEDITERRANEAN GREEK PESTO PIZZA

We are bringing this one to you all the way from Greece. This wonderful delight is something you would make on a nice movie night. Crispy crust, simple and quick and great to eat.

Prep Time: 5 Minutes

Cook Time: 10 Minutes

Servings: 6

Ingredients:

- 2 tbsp. cooking spray (or olive oil)
- 1 poun d fresh pizza dough
- 1/3 cu p marinara sauce
- 1 tbsp. garlic powder
- 1/2 tomato (sliced)
- 12 oz. fresh mozzarella (shredded)
- ¼ cup black olives (sliced)
- ¼ cup feta cheese
- 3 pepperoncini's
- 2 oz. shaved ham
- Tzatziki sauce (to dip)

Directions:

- Divide the pizza dough into 6 sections.

- Plug in the panini press and make sure it's set to lay flat.
- Tear a sheet of aluminum foil, the same size of your panini press.
- Brush or spray the oil on the foil sheet.
- Stretch 1 piece of dough into a round shape. May have to repeat for the dough has elastic features.
- Spread two to three tablespoons of marinara sauce on the stretched dough.
- Sprinkle the garlic powder, tomatoes, ham, black olives, feta cheese, pepperoncini's and last top with cheese.
- Put the foil on the panini press. Close the lid, allowing the upper plate to hover about 1 inch above the pizza. (if you don't have a panini press that has adjustable height, you might try balling up some foil 1-inch spacers by).
- Grill the pizza until the dough is cooked, cheese is melted/bubbly and lightly brown. About 6 to 8 minutes.
- Slice and serve. Make sure you're use the Tzatziki sauce (to dip)

161

CARIBBEAN GRILLED JERK CHICKEN BOWLS

Ingredients:
- ½ cup pineapple juice
- 1 cup prepared jerk chicken marinade
- ½ tsp salt
- 1 tbsp brown sugar
- 2 ears fresh corn, silk removed
- 1 green pepper sliced into quarters
- 4 tbsp toasted almonds
- 1 red pepper sliced into quarters
- 5 tbsp red wine vinegar
- ¼ cup extra virgin olive oil
- 1 cup canned black beans, drained
- 4 cup mixed leafy greens
- 4 4 oz boneless, skinless chicken breasts
- ½ red onion sliced into rings

Instructions:
- Preheat the grill over medium-high heat.
- Place the onions in a foil package.
- Spray all other vegetables, lightly, with olive oil spray.
- Place vegetables in a roasting pan or directly on the grill and

grill until cooked (it takes about 10 minutes for corn to roast "naked").

•Remove all vegetables from the grill, except for the onions, and cook the chicken to about 425-450F.

•Grill for 10 minutes, turning once, or until the internal temperature reaches 165 degrees F.

•Now assemble your bowls.

•Divide mixed greens evenly among 4 large bowls.

•Slice the corn on the cob and divide between the 4 bowls.

•Top with black beans, roasted vegetables, pineapple, and rotisserie chicken.

•In a blender, combine the pineapple juice, olive oil, red wine vinegar, brown sugar, and salt.

•Blend for a few seconds and drizzle the desired amount of pineapple vinaigrette over salads before serving.

•Top with toasted almonds.

162

PEANUT AND JELLY PIZZA

The kiddo's just love this one! Let the kids help you with this delightful dish. It is one that will keep them smiling for a little while and yummy for their tummy!

Prep Time: 5 Minutes

Cook Time: 10 Minutes

Servings: 6

Ingredients:

• 2 tbsp. cooking spray (or olive oil)
• 1 poun d fresh pizza dough
• 1/3 cu p peanut butter
• 1/3 cup of jam (any flavor)
• ½ tsp. cinnamon

Directions:

• Divide the pizza dough into 6 sections.
• Plug in the panini press and make sure it's set to lay flat.
• Tear a sheet of aluminum foil, the same size of your panini press.
• Brush or spray the oil on the foil sheet.
• Stretch 1 piece of dough into a round shape. May have to repeat for the dough has elastic features.

• Spread the peanut butter, then jelly on the stretched dough. Sprinkle the cinnamon on top lightly.

• Put the foil on the panini press. Close the lid, allowing the upper plate to hover about 1 inch above the pizza. (if you don't have a panini press that has adjustable height, you might try balling up some foil 1-inch spacers by).

• Grill the pizza until the dough is cooked, bubbly and lightly brown. The crust may bubble. About 2 to 3 minutes. Let it cool, slice and serve.

163

GRILLED CAJUN CHICKEN DRY RUB SEASONING

Ingredients:
- •2 tablespoons olive oil
- •4 boneless, skinless chicken breasts

Cajun Spice Seasoning :
- •1/2 teaspoon cayenne pepper
- •3/4 teaspoon salt
- •1/2 teaspoon black pepper
- •1/2 teaspoon dried oregano
- •1/4 teaspoon crushed red pepper
- •1/2 teaspoon onion powder
- •1/2 teaspoon dried thyme
- •1 teaspoon garlic powder
- •1 teaspoon paprika

Instructions:
- •Heat a grill over medium-high heat.
- •Place the chicken breasts on a baking sheet or large plate and pat dry. Drizzle lightly with olive oil and rub the chicken to coat it evenly.
- •In a small bowl, combine all the spices and stir well. Sprinkle half of the spice mixture over the top of the chicken breasts, turn

the chicken over, and sprinkle the remaining half of the spice mixture over the bottom of each breast so that the chicken is evenly coated with the Cajun seasoning.

•Place the chicken breasts directly on the hot side of the grill and grill for approximately 5-6 minutes per side, depending on the thickness of your chicken, until the internal temperature of the breasts reaches 160 degrees using a thermometer. instant read meat. You can also check if the chicken is done by making a small cut in the thickest part to see if it is opaque in the center, or by pressing the thick end of the chicken with your finger to see if there is any resistance. If chicken is done, take away from the grill and allow to stand for 5 minutes.

•Use whole chicken breasts on grilled Cajun chicken sandwiches or slice them up and add to a grilled Cajun chicken salad or creamy pasta dishes.

GRILLED PINEAPPLE CHEESECAKE PARFAIT

Ingredients:
- 1 sleeve graham crackers, crushed
- 1 pineapple cut into spears

Cheesecake Filling :
- 2 cups heavy whipping cream
- 4¼ oz pkg Cheesecake flavor instant pudding

Instructions:

•Turn the Hamilton Beach Indoor Broiler Grill to 350 degrees. When done, place pineapple stalks on grill surface.

• Grill on each side until golden brown and caramelized. Remove to the cutting board and cut into small pieces.

•For the cheesecake filling: use a cold metal bowl and beaters. Pour pudding mix and heavy whipping cream into cold bowl, beat over high heat until thick and creamy. Approximately 2 minutes. It will have a thicker consistency than pudding.

•Layer in a glass (or bowl if you don't do it individual): graham crackers, roasted pineapple and cheesecake filling.

•Garnish with additional roasted pineapple and crushed graham crackers if desired.

HUNGRY GRILLED ROMAINE SALAD

Ingredients:
- •2 dashes each salt and pepper
- •2 tbsp. fresh basil finely chopped
- •2 tbsp. Balsamic Vinegar
- •1 large heart romaine lettuce halved lengthwise
- •1/4 cup red onion diced
- •1 tbsp. Extra Virgin Olive Oil
- •1/4 cup reduced-fat feta cheese crumbled
- •1/4 cup tomato diced

Instructions:
- •Bring the grill to high heat.
- •Spray and brush 1/2 tsp. olive oil on the cut sides of each romaine half. Sprinkle with salt and pepper.
- • Place the romaine lettuce halves on the grill, cut sides down. Grill until slightly charred, 1-2 minutes.
- •Place the romaine lettuce halves, cut side up. Top with tomato, onion, cheese, and basil.
- •In a small bowl, whisk together the vinegar and the remaining 2 teaspoons of olive oil. Spray and enjoy!

GRILLED MAHI MAHI TACOS WITH CHIPOTLE CREAM SAUCE

Ingredients:
- 4 fresh Mahi Mahi filets or frozen, thawed (about 4 oz each)
- 1 tbsp coconut sugar
- ½ cup low-fat sour cream
- ½ tbsp extra virgin olive oil
- ¼ cup mild to hot pickled jalapeños depending on your preference
- ½ head red cabbage shredded
- 1-2 tsp adobo seasoning blend to taste
- 5.3 oz plain Greek yogurt
- 8 corn tortillas
- 2-3 chipotle peppers in adobo sauce depending on your heat preference
- 4 ⅓ tbsp fresh lime juice

Instructions:
- Preheat the oven to 350 degrees F.
- First, make the chipotle cream sauce.
- Place the yogurt, sour cream, chipotle peppers, 1 teaspoon lemon juice, and coconut sugar in a blender and blend until smooth. Pour into a bowl and reserve.

•Preheat the grill over medium-high heat (we used a Big Green Egg and heated it to 400 degrees F)

•In a shallow dish, pour 1 tablespoon of fresh lemon juice over each browning fillet, cover, and place in the refrigerator to marinate for 15 minutes while the grill heats up.

•Shred the cabbage and reserve.

•Drizzle the fish with olive oil, rub with marinade, and lightly season with salt and pepper.

•Cook Mahi Mahi in a grill pan, turning every 5 minutes until the steaks are flaky but not falling apart (approximately 15 to 20 minutes, depending on the size of your steaks)

•As soon as the fish goes to the grill, wrap the tortillas in 2 stacks of 4 in aluminum foil.

•Heat in the oven for 15-20 minutes, while the fish is cooking.

•Assemble the tacos, using ½ fillet per taco, top with shredded cabbage, pickled jalapeños, and drizzle with chipotle cream.

167

GRILLED POBLANO PEPPER
SOUTHWEST BURGERS

Ingredients:

Southwest Burgers :
- •1 teaspoon Freshly ground black pepper
- • Lettuce
- •2 tablespoons olive oil
- •Sliced red onion
- •Sliced tomatoes
- •6 Good hamburger buns
- •1 1/2 teaspoon kosher salt
- •6 slices Sharp cheddar cheese
- •2 pounds ground chuck
- •4 poblano peppers

Chipotle Aioli :
- •1 clove garlic, minced
- •2/3 cup olive oil
- •1/2 teaspoon dry mustard
- •1 chipotle pepper in adobo sauce, minced
- •1/2 teaspoon kosher salt
- •Juice of 1/2 a lemon
- •2 egg yolks

Instructions:

•Grill the poblano peppers by first rubbing them with a little olive oil. Heat the grill over medium-high heat, then place the whole poblano peppers over an indirect heat area (turn off burners if necessary, or rearrange the coals so that the peppers are not directly on the heat source) and close the lid. so they can be roasted for 10-15 minutes. Flip once or twice to make sure all sides are cooked evenly and the peppers begin to blister.

•Move the peppers to direct heat and grill until the skin is burned, turning to get all the sides of the peppers. Transfer to a plate or plate and cover tightly with plastic wrap for 10 minutes until cool enough to handle. Peel the charred skin from the peppers and slice them open to remove the seeds and stem. Cut the poblano peppers into large slices to coat your southwestern burgers.

•Alternatively, preheat the oven broiler to high heat, then place the poblano peppers on a foil-lined baking sheet and roast about 8 minutes, turning occasionally, until blackened, then continue to sweat the peppers as described above.

•To make the burgers, split the meat into 6 equivalent slices. Gently shape patties that are slightly larger than the size of the buns you plan to use, about 3/4 inch thick. Make a hole in the middle of individual patty with your thumb and spice both rims of individual patty with salt and freshly ground black pepper.

•Heat grill over medium-high heat, then place patties directly over flames or heat source and grill, covered, 3-4 minutes per side for patties that are medium-raw to medium. If you prefer your burgers to be closer to medium to medium well cooked, cook them for 4-5 minutes on each side. During the last few minutes of grilling, top the patties with the sliced cheese to melt and toast the buns.

•Allow patties to rest 3-4 minutes after removing from grill so juices can redistribute before serving.

•Assemble the burgers by placing a piece of lettuce on top of the toasted bottom bun, followed by the burger with melted cheese, poblano pepper slices, tomato slices, onion, and the toasted top bun that has been generously slathered with chipotle aioli.

Chipotle Aioli :

•Combine all of the aioli ingredients except olive oil in a food processor or blender and process for 20 seconds.

•With the food processor running, very slowly drizzle the oil in a fine stream into the egg yolk mixture, taking about 2 minutes to pour it all in, until fully incorporated and the aioli is emulsified.

•Refrigerate until ready to use.

GRILLED HALIBUT WITH TOMATO AVOCADO RELISH

Ingredients:
- 1 tsp pepper
- 1 tbsp fresh parsley finely chopped
- 1 tsp white wine vinegar
- 10 oz Wild-Caught Halibut filets (about 2- 5 oz filets)
- 1 cup chopped fresh tomatoes
- 2 tbsp fresh lemon juice
- 1 avocado peeled, seeded and diced
- $\frac{1}{4}$ tsp garlic salt
- 3 tbsp olive oil

Instructions:
- Preheat the grill to medium-high heat.
- Combine 2 tablespoons of olive oil, 1 tablespoon of lemon juice, vinegar, tomatoes, avocado, parsley, $\frac{1}{2}$ teaspoon of pepper, and garlic salt in a small bowl.
- Toss to coat and set aside the sauce.
- Mix the remaining olive oil and the tablespoon of lemon juice and brush the halibut fillets to coat
- Season with the remaining $\frac{1}{2}$ teaspoon pepper and a pinch of salt.

•Broil 6 to 8 minutes, flip and broil 5 more minutes until fish flakes with a fork

•Top with seasoning and serve immediately.

Lightning Source UK Ltd.
Milton Keynes UK
UKHW021337230221
379243UK00001BB/86